SUCCESS WITH

)

ock.

·ck.

SUCCESS WITH
CLEMATIS

Marigold Badcock

GUILD OF MASTER CRAFTSMAN
PUBLICATIONS LIMITED

First published 2005 by
Guild of Master Craftsman Publications Ltd,
Castle Place, 166 High Street, Lewes,
East Sussex, BN7 1XU

Illustrations (line drawings) by John Yates

ISBN 1 86108 407 2

The publishers and author can accept no legal responsibility for any
consequences arising from the application of information, advice or
instructions given in this publication.

A catalogue record of this book is available from the British Library.

Production Manager: Hilary MacCallum
Managing Editor: Gerrie Purcell
Project Editor: Dominique Page

Designed by John Hawkins
Set in Futura

Colour origination Altaimage Ltd
Printed and bound by Kyodo Printing, Singapore

To Kelly, with her passion for flowers,
and Stuart, always a lover of nature
and now finding the joy of a garden.

Contents

Introduction

Clematis must surely rate as one of the most beautiful of the climbing vines, and with such a vast array of colours, shapes and forms on offer, the choice is almost endless. The problem with having so much choice is where to begin. You may be drawn to the large cultivars, which are available in a myriad of colours, from bold purples and reds to shades of pink or purest white. Maybe the smaller-flowered, but equally beautiful, range of viticellas are more to your taste. There are evergreens with delicate, fern-like foliage, nodding bright yellow bells of *orientalis*; tulip-shaped *texensis* or the simple, tiny stars of *vitalba* (virgin's bower). Clematis to climb, clematis to scramble – not only is it hard to choose, but how does one choose wisely?

It is not so long ago that clematis were considered to be difficult to grow and to care for. Fortunately, as a deeper understanding of their cultural needs developed and breeders produced a wide range of plants more resistant to attack from wilt their popularity soared, and now many gardeners are enjoying a succession of clematis throughout the seasons.

There are over 250 known species of clematis – pronounced klem-e-tis – native to northern and southern hemispheres, and a constantly growing choice of cultivated hybrids. Within these pages I will help you to understand the cultural needs of the three different groups, how to choose, plant, prune and look after your clematis, plus offer suggestions for companion planting and ideas for alternative supports.

Soon, with growing confidence, you too may become a collector with a wide range of species and cultivars to enjoy throughout the seasons, because your garden, no matter how large or small, will always find room for one more clematis.

LEFT 'Arctic Queen' an early flowering hybrid will produce a mass of fully double blooms in late spring

11

CHAPTER 1

Where to grow clematis

One of the greatest advantages of clematis is how little space they take relative to their flowering impact. No matter how much land you have, whether it is acres or a tiny garden, clematis can play a major role in enhancing the plants and structures that you have available. For instance, with the assistance of some trellis or wire supports, house walls, pergolas, archways and fences can be transformed. Natural supports can be offered by way of trees, shrubs and other climbers, while with the aid of simple tripods or special structures, height and colour can be added to borders. And finally, where better to enjoy clematis than planted in containers on the patio or deck where they can offer a long succession of blooms to complement your other plants?

ABOVE **Spiraea provides shelter for** *Clematis* **'Arabella'**

ABOVE 'Hagley Hybrid' should be grown in semi-shade to protect the delicate colour from fading

CHOOSING A SUITABLE SITE

Clematis are much hardier than their fragile beauty suggests. Many varieties are able to withstand prolonged periods of frost and snow during their dormant season, even to as low as −30°F (−34.4°C). (One of the most dangerous times for clematis, however, is when the ground starts to warm up and the young shoots emerge: cut back by frost they can often take a considerable while to recover.) Nonetheless, it is still important to research the clematis you have in mind and to choose the most suitable site for it, as some will only really flourish in warm, sheltered aspects while others will grow happily in semi-shade. Semi-shade is especially suitable for pale pink and delicate shades which often fade in strong sunlight.

As a brief guide, many of the evergreens, such as the winter-flowering *cirrhosa* which originates from the warm climate of southern Europe, are unable to withstand long periods of sub-zero temperatures and may not grow readily in the colder north.

Spring-flowering *armandii*, from southern China, with its large, leathery evergreen leaves, will reluctantly tolerate short periods of frost, drooping in discomfort, and then buck up when warmer weather returns.

The Atragene group, which includes the *alpinas* from mainland Europe and the *macropetalas* from China, seem to be quite adaptable to the cold.

The *montanas*, found growing to great heights over trees in the Himalayas, are now grown extensively in moderate climate zones.

Viticellas and resulting hybrids have done a marvellous job adapting away from Spanish soil, as has the beautiful tulip-shaped *texensis* which was discovered growing wild and scrambling through the scrubland of Texas.

The orange bells of *tanguitica*, originating, from north-west India and China, and the similar *orientalis* from Afghanistan, are firm favourites in most regions of Europe and the United States.

In many cases, however, cross-breeding has not only made it difficult to assess parentage but it has also created a new tolerance that enables the plants to survive and flourish in conditions that are far removed from their original habitat.

When choosing clematis you will not only need to consider the climate of your region, but also your position within it; for instance, although you may live in a cold climate, your home might dwell within a valley that is warmed by southerly winds. Or, you may have your own microclimate in certain areas of the garden, such as a south-facing wall or perhaps a strategically placed hedge or fence.

For those living in a climate that generally has long sunny days and hard baked soil, natural shade may exist or can be created, and the soil mixed with enough friable and moisture-retentive material to provide the growing conditions that are so beloved by clematis. In regions of infrequent rainfall, regular watering is essential.

In general, when seeking the best conditions, clematis appreciate friable, moist soil with their feet planted in the shade, their heads in the sun and sufficient support for their coiling tendrils to cling to. A secure support will help to minimize the effects of the wind, which not only breaks their vulnerable stems but also loosens the roots on which the plant relies for succour.

With combination planting, the host plant can often provide the shade, shelter and support that the clematis needs, but you must also bear in mind that it will compete for nourishment and moisture, and unless you compensate for this, the hungry clematis or host plant will suffer.

LEFT *Clematis montana* has plenty of room along this garden wall and provides a lovely backcloth for mimosa

ABOVE **Planting a clematis so that it will grow into a shrub that is already well established**

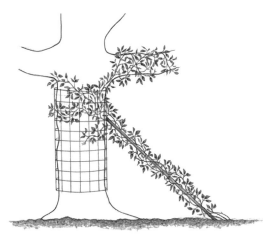

ABOVE **Planting a clematis so that it will grow up the trunk and into the branches of a tree**

ABOVE **Wire mesh wrapped loosely around the trunk enables** *macropetala* **to climb up to the branches of the tree**

Where it is possible to create the desired conditions, clematis will often settle and provide long and valuable service within quite a diverse range of weather conditions. If in doubt about the right clematis for a specific location, seek advice from your local nursery or specialist grower who will be able to provide you with a list of recommended clematis for your region. You may then decide to experiment further, even if it means a disappointment or two.

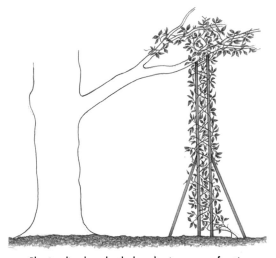

ABOVE **Planting directly under the branches is one way of getting clematis into a tree**

16

GROWING THROUGH SUPPORT PLANTS

If you would like your clematis to climb a shrub, choose a position where its roots will be shaded for most of the day. Do not plant it too close, because the shrub may take the greater share of the moisture and nutrients from the soil. Also, clematis roots need lots of space in which to develop. Use a few canes, twigs or branches to train the clematis across to the shrub. A few twisty ties will help to anchor it so that it does not get blown off course. Keep an eye out as it grows and continue to encourage it to stay with its partner; clematis are quite fickle and they will happily wind themselves around foxgloves and delphiniums or any other nearby plant.

The ideal way to grow clematis up a tree is to plant them at the same time so that they grow together; this is how the rampant wild species around the world grow to such incredible heights. However, a little more work is required if you would like to grow clematis up an existing tree. If you want the flowers to decorate the trunk as well as the branches, the clematis will need some means of support; wire netting or a wire grid attached to the trunk is the best way to achieve this. The planting hole should be dug at least 2ft (60cm) away from the base of the tree and the clematis trained to it along a cane. Alternatively, the clematis can be planted on the northern side of the tree, under the periphery of the branches, and supported by stout canes or poles to reach them.

TRELLIS

Clematis cannot climb unless their tendrils have something to cling to; they are unable to grow onto a wall or fence without some additional means of support. They require a trellis or wires fashioned into a grid.

Wooden trellis is available in conventional square or diamond shapes, and as they come in a range of different colours they can make attractive features in their own right. This is an important consideration for the winter months when the beautiful blooms are not there for decoration, especially so in the small garden where every feature needs to be very carefully considered. Plastic-covered wire trellis is only suitable for small areas and is not as strong as wood. As the intention is for the clematis to stay for many years, I think it is worth investing in the strongest and most attractive means of support within your budget.

Air should be allowed to flow freely around the clematis and this will not be the case if the trellis is fixed directly onto the wall or fence; it needs to be proud. This can be achieved by first fixing wooden battens onto the wall and then screwing the trellis onto these. If you also fix corresponding battens onto the trellis, the bottom pair can be hinged together and the top pair fixed with hooks and eyes, thus enabling the whole thing to be unhooked and lowered to the ground. This allows easy access to the wall or fence for decorating or fresh preservative to be applied to the trellis.

Trellis can also be purchased in trompe-l'oeil style and when placed on a wall will create the illusion of an archway. The effect can be further enhanced by painting the centre of the archway in a different colour from the surrounding wall or

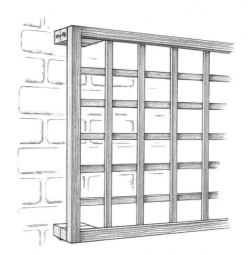

ABOVE **A hinged trellis can be lowered from the wall for any necessary maintenance**

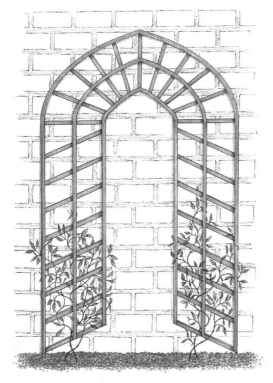

ABOVE **Trompe l'oeil trellis**

RIGHT **A strong wire grid provides excellent support for climbers on this large boundary wall**

by filling it with mirrored glass. The latter is ideal for a small courtyard garden, where it will create the illusion of space as it reflects plants and light.

Clematis will look very effective growing around the outer archway, but do not choose a rampant variety or the effect will be lost.

WALLS AND FENCES WITH VINE EYES AND WIRE

While it may not look quite as attractive as wooden trellis, strong wire that has been threaded between vine eyes – screws with a loop at the end – will provide you with an inexpensive and effective alternative. The wires should be spaced approximately 12in (30cm) apart horizontally and vertically, thereby

ABOVE **It is important to plant the clematis the correct distance from the wall so that it isn't sheltered from the rain**

ABOVE **C. viticella 'Margot Koster' has been trained to cover the upright of this pergola at RHS Rosemoor, Devon, south-west England**

creating a square grid. Brick and concrete walls will need to be drilled and plugged to hold the vine eyes. Buy the longest ones you can, so that the wire is held away from the wall, thus allowing air to circulate freely around the plant.

When planting clematis to decorate the walls of a house or boundary, do not go too close to the structure; the soil there is often very dry because it has been shielded from the rain. Plant 2ft (60cm) away and train the clematis on canes or sticks towards the wall or fence. This method will help to prevent the clematis roots from becoming too dry.

PERGOLAS AND ARBOURS

A pergola over a pathway or an arbour that is positioned in a secluded part of the garden where you can sit peacefully and while away an hour or two, will not only make lovely features but also provide an opportunity to grow clematis and other climbing plants.

When planning a pergola or an arbour, make sure that it is both high and wide enough to allow you to walk or sit beneath it without brushing up against the plants. This is especially important when growing roses because their thorns can be quite painful. If the plan is to grow roses and clematis together, then the rose should be trained around the upright; it will then provide a natural support for the clematis. Encourage the clematis to twine around the lower branches, otherwise it will bolt straight up.

Clematis that are grown on their own or with other less woody climbers will need additional means of support if they are to climb the poles. Strands of wire wrapped around and tacked into place are not really adequate unless you are prepared to spend time tying the new growth to them regularly. Plastic-coated wire trellis provides a greater means of support. It also bends quite easily and can be stapled or nailed into position. Square-grid wire netting is alternative option.

ABOVE **A rose trained along a rope between the uprights of a pergola provides a very attractive feature**

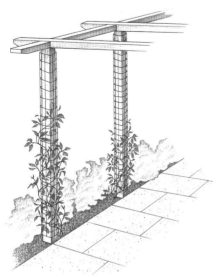

ABOVE **The clematis needs a grid-wire support to climb over the pergola successfully**

Wooden trellis can be fixed between the uprights of an arbour to provide effective support for plants as they spread, and a little three-sided house of plants like this looks wonderful when covered with sweet-smelling climbers and a mass of clematis blooms.

FREE-STANDING SUPPORTS

Obelisks and tripods can be used to great effect in the border and on the patio. Tripods can be inserted into large tubs or barrels to provide support for the smaller varieties of clematis. They can be purchased in wood and wrought iron, the latter being elegant if somewhat expensive.

A simple framework to set in a border can be made out of three rustic poles 6–7ft (1.8–2.1m) long, set in a triangle. Nine crossbars can be made out of the same type of poles sawn in half.

21

ABOVE *Clematis* 'Mrs Cholmondley', beautifully supported on a simple rustic structure

ABOVE **A three-sided support made from rustic poles and covered with a clematis makes an attractive feature in the border**

One pole should provide six crossbars of 24in (60cm) in length. A timber merchant will usually be willing to cut them to size ready for you to nail or to screw together. Simple free-standing structures such as this can be successfully used to create height in areas where it is otherwise lacking.

Another simple and very effective support can be made by placing a 6½ft (2m) fence post into a Met post inserted into the ground, or by simply cementing the post into the ground. The post should be 6ft (1.8m) above ground level. Encase the post in a column made of four pieces of 1 x 6ft (30cm x 1.8m) trellis nailed together then screw or nail the trellis to the post in one corner.

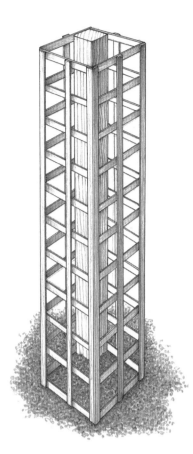

ABOVE **A support made from trellis attached to an upright post secured in the ground**

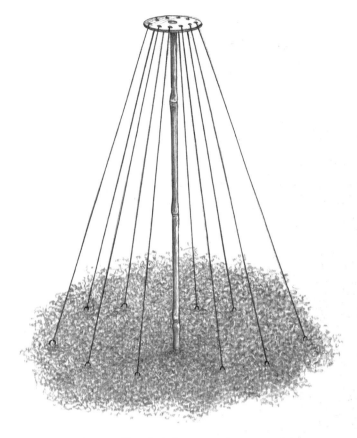

ABOVE **A clematis will happily climb a wigwam of wires suspended from a bean pole**

Bean and pea supports in the shape of a wigwam can now be purchased, and at the end of the season they can be lifted and stored in the shed for the winter months. A support such as this is quite adequate for one or two small clematis, especially those varieties that are hard pruned annually, because the support can be put back in place before the growing season starts.

A very similar structure can be made with a 7ft (2.1m) cane. Push the cane into the ground. Slip a runner bean cane top over the end of the cane and attach strong, plastic-coated wire to the holes. Tie the ends of the wires to tent pegs and push these firmly into the ground to create a circle. The result should look like a maypole before the dancing begins.

GROWING CLEMATIS IN CONTAINERS

Container gardening has become increasingly popular as people extend their homes into the garden with smartly dressed terraces and patios. For the small garden particularly, pots and tubs are invaluable, because they can be planted with the best of the current season's offerings and simply placed wherever they will make the most impact. Many gardeners are now seeking unusual plants and combinations to enhance the lovely containers that are available in an ever-increasing variety of materials, shapes and colours. Containers provide an ideal opportunity to grow clematis of a more tender variety, because they can be moved into a frost-free area for the winter.

23

TYPES OF CONTAINERS

Many disappointing results are experienced due to planting clematis in containers that are too small. This is quite understandable, because it is not that easy to find containers that measure as large as 18in (45cm) deep with a 12in (30cm) diameter, but this is the ideal size in which to grow one or possibly two small clematis. Large wooden half barrels and Versailles-style planters generally fall short of the required depth, but usually compensate by having a larger diameter. If you are handy at do-it-yourself or perhaps 'know someone who can', you can make a wooden container that is 18in (45cm) deep and 18in (45cm) square in which to grow two or more clematis and a few supporting plants, or a shrub over which the clematis can tumble.

Very large terracotta pots look attractive, but make sure that they are frost hardy. Ali Baba shapes might be striking but unfortunately are not that practical, as it is difficult to replace the top soil annually and even more difficult to remove the plant without damaging it when you need to replace the soil completely.

Stone containers of the required size are prohibitively expensive but will last virtually forever and make a superb, permanent feature. Also readily available are concrete lookalikes but unfortunately, and despite new and vastly improved technology, they never quite meet the visual impact of the real thing. Nonetheless they make a good, sturdy, long-lasting alternative. The problem with both of these materials is their weight. They are almost impossible to move once they have been filled.

There has been a vast improvement recently in the quality of plastic containers, which come in all shapes, sizes and finishes. The advantage of plastic is that it is lightweight and has good insulating properties.

Select your container with care. If you want to grow clematis successfully, it is best to think big.

Preparing, planting and maintaining containers

- When buying clematis, choose varieties that are suitable for growing in containers; for example, containers are not suitable for the very rampant varieties.

- Wooden containers should always be treated with a safe proprietary preservative before planting commences.

- Line the sides, but not the bottom, of the container with insulating material; this will help to keep the roots cool in summer and warm in winter. One way is to line it with tin foil, shiny side to the container, and then add a 1in (2.5cm) layer of newspaper; another is to use heavy-duty plastic or bubble wrap.

- Make sure there are sufficient drainage holes or the plant will become waterlogged.

- Site the container in the required position. Ensure that the aspect suits the chosen clematis and companion plants, if there are any. Use bricks, blocks or battens to raise the container off the ground to assist free drainage.

- Place a good layer of broken pots, stones or pebbles into the base of the container, again to aid drainage.

- Mix together a half quantity of fertile friable soil with half compost, or use a commercial, soil-based compost like John Innes No. 2.

Add two handfuls of bonemeal and a tablespoonful of general fertilizer, such as Growmore, and fill the container to within 2in (5cm) of the rim.

- The clematis will need support if it is to climb. There are special metal or wooden obelisks available from suppliers that look very attractive. However, if these are beyond your budget, you can insert three or more canes around the diameter of the container and tie them at the top in a wigwam style or fan them out (see illustration below). Alternatively, place the container against a wall or fence onto which trellis has been fixed. The clematis is then simply trained from the container to the trellis.

- Plant the clematis deeply to encourage new shoots to form.

- Water the container thoroughly and finish off with a 2in (5cm) layer of small pebbles or bark to retain moisture.

- Water regularly: once daily during the growing season, twice daily during hot and dry conditions. Never allow the container to become dry at any time of year. If the surface is dry for a depth of 1–1¾in (1–2cm), water is needed. Do not overwater clematis; the soil should be moist all through but not sodden, otherwise nutrients will be washed away and the roots will become over-saturated.

- Feed the clematis regularly during the growing season with a potash-based fertilizer but stop as soon as the flowers begin to open or their season will be shortened. If the clematis is of a variety that blooms in the early summer and again later, then feed between flushes to encourage a heavier crop of flowers.

SUGGESTED CLEMATIS FOR CONTAINERS

Alpina types, such as: 'Constance', 'Pink Flamingo' and 'Francis Rivis'.
Macropetala types, such as: *C. macropetala*, 'Markhams Pink' and 'White Swan'.
Early large-flowered cultivars, such as: 'Barbara Jackman', 'Gillian Blades', 'H.F. Young', 'Miss Bateman', 'Special Occasion' and 'Wada's Primrose'.
Viticellas, such as: *Alba Luxurians*, 'Madame Julia Correvon' and 'Minuet'.
Late large-flowered cultivars, such as: *Florida Alba Plena*, *Florida Sieboldii*, 'Hagley Hybrid', 'Prince Charles' and 'Rouge Cardinal'.
Texensis types, such as: 'Duchess of Albany', 'Gravetye Beauty' and 'Princess Diana'.
Late small-flowered species and cultivars, such as: *Crispa*, *Fusca* and *Viorna*.

ABOVE **Lining provides valuable insulation in a container**

25

CHAPTER 2

Growing clematis

Having explored your garden to see where clematis can be planted for best effect, it is important that you choose clematis that will not only enhance the colour scheme of your garden but will also be of the desired height and spread. The A–Z directory on pages 112 to 153 will help you to select just the right clematis for each location you have in mind.

The aim is to have strong and healthy plants that are covered in a multitude of magnificent blooms, so when buying clematis make sure that the plant has a good root system and that the leaves are vigorous. In this chapter I will explain how to plant your clematis to give them the best start in life in your garden, how to nurture and care for them and how to keep pests and diseases at bay. I will also give ideas on effective means of support for the plants, how to train them through shrubs and trees and how to succeed when planting into containers.

THE SOIL

A vigorous and healthy plant producing a mass of lovely blooms for many years will reward the time and effort you bestow in providing the best conditions for it at the planting stage. Clematis do not appear to be fussy as to whether the soil is alkaline or acid, but they do need fertile, well-drained, humus-rich loam.

PLANTING

First dig a hole that is at least 12in (30cm) across and 18in (45cm) deep. Fill the bottom 8in (20cm) with a planting mixture consisting of one part fibrous, well-rotted compost, one part topsoil, and three handfuls of bonemeal for each barrow load.

Until recently, the advice from specialists was to plant clematis 4in (10cm) below the surface to encourage the submerged buds to grow into new stems. This was an insurance against the existing stems developing stem rot, or clematis wilt as it is also known (more about this later). This method of deep planting can also provide protection during harsh winter conditions. New theories suggest that deep planting may be counterproductive in the endeavour to avoid stem rot, because it does not allow a free flow of air around the lower buds, thus allowing fungal spores to develop. Until more evidence has been accumulated, we can only presume that deep planting in cold areas will protect the roots and conventional planting in mild districts will enable free-flowing air. Whichever you choose, to encourage the production of new stems and strong growth every clematis should be pruned down to the lowest pair of healthy buds in the first late winter after planting. This will delay flowering on clematis that form flowers on the previous year's growth, but it is the most effective way of encouraging the production of new shoots and strong growth.

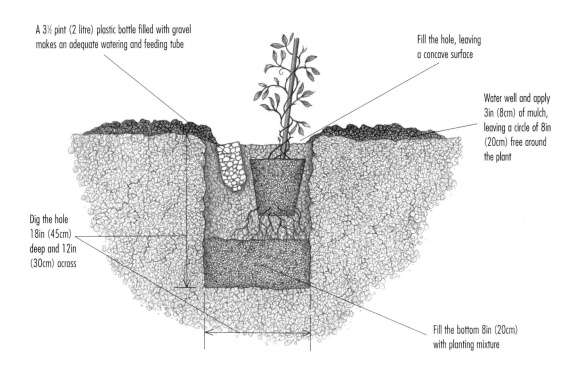

A 3½ pint (2 litre) plastic bottle filled with gravel makes an adequate watering and feeding tube

Fill the hole, leaving a concave surface

Water well and apply 3in (8cm) of mulch, leaving a circle of 8in (20cm) free around the plant

Dig the hole 18in (45cm) deep and 12in (30cm) across

Fill the bottom 8in (20cm) with planting mixture

Before filling the hole, insert a feeding tube to aid watering and feeding of the root system. A 3½ pint (2 litre) plastic bottle with the base cut off, filled with gravel and placed into the hole, neck down, works well and usually lasts long enough for the plant to become deep rooted before the container finally perishes. Remember to remove the screw-on lid. A length of heavy-duty plastic tubing, the type used for downpipes, will provide a more permanent feeding tube.

Fill the hole with good-quality topsoil mixed with compost. Firm the soil around the plant, leaving a slightly concave surface, and water thoroughly. Then apply 3in (8cm) of mulching to keep the surface cool. Garden compost is ideal, or you can use mushroom compost, moist peat, leaf mould or bark. Leave a circle 8in (20cm) free of mulch around the plant to avoid rotting the stem, and check that the feeding tube is not covered.

WATERING AND FEEDING

Clematis are particularly hungry and thirsty plants, therefore a feeding tube will help to get water and nourishment to the root system. Water regularly, especially during the first season when the roots are becoming established. In very dry weather, 1 gallon (5 litres) per plant each day is not an excessive amount.

Feed weekly during the growing season with a liquid fertilizer that is high in potash and diluted to the manufacturer's recommendations. Do not give liquid fertilizer when the clematis is in bloom, as this will shorten the flowering period. However, do continue with the watering programme. A handful of bonemeal around each plant in the autumn, gently worked into the soil, will provide a slow-release fertilizer to encourage root growth. This is also a good time to top up the mulching.

PRUNING

The two things that are most likely to deter people from buying clematis are 'clematis wilt', which we will cover later, and the perceived difficulties related to pruning.

While it is not quite as simple as the adage 'bloom before June, no need to prune', if you have inherited a number of clematis and do not even know their names let alone their pruning requirements, you will not go far wrong if you live by this maxim. It would seem that the earlier clematis come into flower, the less pruning they require, but pruning clematis and training them in accordance with their needs is essential if we are to enjoy them at their best. All too often we see clematis growing on one stem with their flowers in a cluster above eye level. What we want to achieve is a healthy plant with a number of shoots and flowers from the bottom to the top. The first step towards achieving this goal is to hard prune all clematis in the first late winter/early

All clematis should be pruned back hard in the late winter/early spring after planting

spring after planting; this will encourage the plant to grow another stem. During spring, as the stems are growing, it is best to pinch some of them out to encourage fan-shaped growth.

ABOVE **Species plants such as this *Clematis macropetala* are more likely to reproduce true to type than hybrids and cultivars**

For pruning purposes, the different kinds of clematis can be divided into three categories:

CATEGORY 1

No pruning required. Flowers are formed on the previous year's growth. Clematis groups in this category are the *cirrhosa*, *armandii*, *alpina*, *macropetala* and *montana*.

Note: If any of the clematis in this category becomes too entangled and overgrown, they can be cut back to a more manageable level after flowering. If the stems are really thick and old, the plant may not recover from the shock if too much is removed at once; it is preferable to tackle the job over two or three seasons.

CATEGORY 2

Light pruning. Flowers are formed on the previous year's growth. In mid-winter, work your way down from the top of each stem to a plump and healthy bud. Prune just above it. Clematis groups in this category are the early and mid-season large-flowered varieties.

Note: The early varieties usually commence flowering in mid- to late spring with a second flush in late summer. If you prune them too heavily you will be short of early flowers. If the blooms are all at the top with few lower down and the clematis has a healthy number of stems, after flowering prune back some of the stems to encourage new growth.

Mid-season varieties usually commence flowering in late spring and continue through to late summer. Here there is the choice of light pruning or hard pruning. Once again, a mixture of both will ensure new growth that can be trained to bear flowers low down.

CATEGORY 3

Hard pruning. Flowers are formed on the current year's growth. In late winter/early spring, from the bottom of the plant and on every stem, work up to a pair of healthy buds and cut just above them. Clematis groups in this category are the late large-flowered hybrids, *viticellas*, *orientalis*, *texensis* and herbaceous varieties.

Note: Clematis of the *orientalis* family can look very effective when grown through large shrubs and small trees, in which case you should cut back some of the stems in late winter to encourage new growth and leave the others to continue their climb. There may come a point after a few years when a complete hard pruning is required.

ABOVE **Light pruning for clematis that bear flowers on the previous year's growth**

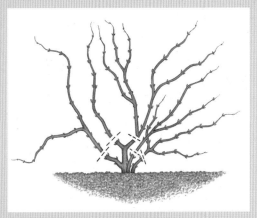

ABOVE **Hard pruning for clematis that bear flowers on the current year's growth**

INCREASING STOCK

For the amateur gardener, the three easiest ways to increase clematis stocks is to grow them from seeds, to take cuttings, or by layering.

GROWING FROM SEEDS

Plants grown from the seeds of species clematis are likely to be similar to the parent plant. Plants grown from hybrid clematis or any of the large-flowered cultivars may turn out to be very different from their parents in size, shape, colour and vigour. You may produce a wonderful new variety or a rather worthless plant. The seeds of species plants seem to be easier to germinate, and if conditions are right you may see the first little shoot in about six weeks. The seeds of large-flowered hybrids may take much longer to germinate. Spring is a good time to sow seeds.

Growing clematis from seed

SOWING THE SEED

- Use 4in (10cm) pots or small seed trays that are not too shallow, because clematis form long roots quite quickly. Fill the pots to within ½in (1cm) of the top with moist, well-drained, soil-based seed compost. Firm the surface lightly.
- Sow the seed evenly; make sure you do not overcrowd. There is no need to remove the fluff from the seed. Sieve a little more compost on top, just to cover the seeds, and add ¼in (5mm) of very coarse sand or grit, which will help to protect the seeds from disturbance.
- Stand the pot in water containing a fungicide until the grit shows clear signs of dampness.
- Label clearly with the name and the date and then place the pots outside or in a cold greenhouse in a well-lit position out of direct sunlight. If they are to be placed outside, protect them from birds, mice and so on by covering them with a sheet of glass or plastic.

- Check periodically to make sure that the compost is moist but not saturated.
- Most clematis will germinate without heat. In fact, many varieties seem to need a cold period prior to germination. Germination may be erratic; they may come all at once or be spread out over several months.

POTTING ON

- It is preferable to let the seedlings reach a height of about 2in (5cm) before you transplant them. Late summer is the best time of year to do this, but if they are not large enough by the autumn, leave them until the following spring.
- Make sure the pot or tray of seedlings is well watered before transplanting them into individual pots that are no smaller than 2½in (6.5cm) deep and containing seed compost. Handle the seedlings gently, holding them by their leaves.
- Tall seedlings can be pinched back. Pinching back should be carried out at each re-potting stage.
- Label each pot with the plant's name.
- Lastly, stand the pot in a sheltered spot in the open garden or alternatively in a cold greenhouse, away from direct sunlight.

Growing clematis from cuttings

Use a sharp knife to cut between the nodes

- Prepare the pots by ensuring that they are thoroughly clean. Fill to within ½in (1cm) of the top with cutting compost. Firm lightly. Add a top layer of coarse sand or grit.
- Cut a length of vine from the mid-section which is neither too soft nor too woody.
- With a clean, sharp blade, cut through the vine immediately above a node and again about 1½in (4cm) below the same node.
- Reduce the foliage by removing all the leaves from one side and cutting any large remaining leaves in half. This will help to reduce moisture loss until the cuttings have become rooted.
- Completely immerse the prepared cuttings in a fungicide mixture. Allow them to drain.
- Dip the base of the cutting into rooting powder and shake off any excess.
- Make holes in the compost with a dibber or pencil and insert the cuttings around the pot. Do not overcrowd; the foliage should

not be touching. The node should be level with the grit or coarse sand.
- Attach a label and water the pots with a fungicide diluted to the manufacturer's recommendation; use a fine spray.
- Place the pots in a propagator or cover them with polythene to create a humid atmosphere. A temperature of 68°F (20°C) will aid rooting, which should take place in about four weeks. Check by gently pulling on a leaf. If it feels firm, the cutting will probably have formed roots.
- Pot the cuttings separately or at least make sure that they are not touching. Grow the plants on for another year before setting them in the garden. Nip the side shoots periodically to encourage strong growth.

Cut away the unnecessary foliage to minimize moisture loss

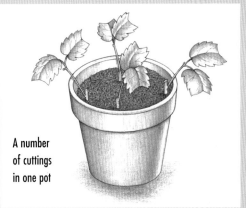

A number of cuttings in one pot

GROWING PLANTS FROM CUTTINGS

An inter-nodal softwood cutting is the method that is recommended for clematis. The best time to take cuttings is mid-spring or early summer.

LAYERING

One of the easiest and most reliable ways of increasing stock is by layering. Clematis usually responds well to this method and when layered in spring will be rooted by autumn.

Layering is undertaken in the bed alongside the parent plant. Because clematis stems are so pliable, a number of plantlets can be produced from a single stem. This is commonly known as 'serpentine layering'.

PESTS AND DISEASES

There is a quite a lot of literature available on the subject of controlling pests and diseases, and gardeners today are becoming increasingly aware of the need to preserve an ecological balance which cannot always be maintained with an excessive use of chemicals. There are a number of pests and diseases that will attack clematis and here we look at some of the ways to control them by chemical and organic methods.

Health and safety is a serious issue for the gardener, especially when using chemicals. When spraying or dusting, make sure you do so in calm weather conditions. It is also wise to protect your eyes and mouth. To avoid spraying,

Serpentine layering

- First, prepare the soil next to the parent plant. The soil should be fertile and friable. If compost is added it should be done three or four weeks beforehand.
- Carefully bend a trailing shoot down to the prepared soil. Trim off the leaves and the side shoots.
- At suitable intervals along the stem, close to the nodes, make several small cuts (not all the way through the stem). Brush these wounds with hormone powder.
- Peg down the wounded sections using U-shaped pieces of wire.
- Separate the plantlets in autumn, by which time the roots should have formed.
- Trim away the old stem and put the new plant into a 5in (13cm) pot of soil-based potting compost.
- Grow on until the plant is established, nipping it back periodically to encourage strong new growth.

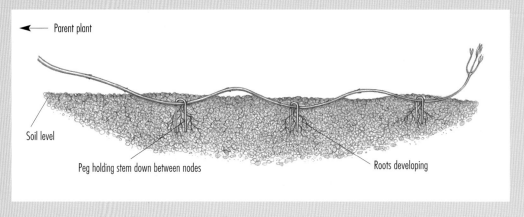

Parent plant

Soil level

Peg holding stem down between nodes

Roots developing

ABOVE **Hoverflies feed on pollen and nectar. A hoverfly larva eats over a thousand aphids during its development**

systemic insecticides and fungicides can be watered into the surrounding soil; the roots will absorb and distribute the chemical up through the rest of the plant. If possible, avoid spraying plants when they are in flower, because certain chemicals can affect bees and hoverflies. If you must spray, do so at dusk when the insects have finished collecting pollen and nectar.

SLUGS AND SNAILS

Unfortunately, these molluscs love clematis, especially those that are young and tender. They can strip a stem and eat young shoots until the plant is decimated or so weakened that it is vulnerable to disease and adverse weather

conditions. Their presence can usually be identified by the slimy trail they leave behind. Slugs are persistent clematis diners all year round. Snails hibernate in the cold weather but are by far the greater climbers; they can scale a wall to incredible heights. Regrettably, they are both so numerous and so persistent that it is virtually impossible to win the battle against them. Do try to keep them at bay when new, young, growth emerges to give the plant a chance to develop a thick, woody stem that is not so easily stripped.

The only really effective deterrent is slug bait, usually sold as pellets, which should be applied in accordance with the manufacturer's instructions.

Pellets scattered around vulnerable plants in late winter/early spring will catch them while they are breeding, minimizing the number of offspring and the repeated use of chemicals. Regular removal of the carcasses will help to prevent them from being eaten by other wildlife; birds and hedgehogs are especially vulnerable. There are little black plastic containers on the market known as 'slug hotels' in which bait is placed and the slugs die, supposedly out of reach of other animals and birds.

There are more ecologically friendly methods that can be tried. A circle of stones around the plant coated in Vaseline can create a slippery barrier which is difficult for slugs and snails to climb. Equally, a barrier of sharp gravel, bark or crushed eggshells may deter them. Ground-up coconut shells are considered to be effective. Many gardeners place a container of beer nearby to which the pests are attracted and drown in a blissful state. However, this may not

ABOVE *Clematis* 'Huldine' has provided a tasty snack for something. The shape of the holes would indicate that earwigs were the culprits

ABOVE **A flowerpot stuffed with straw provides a daytime refuge for earwigs. They can then be disposed of before they start their nightly forage for food**

be until they have dined on a first course of tender young clematis shoots. Unfortunately, it can also be a trap for beneficial wildlife, such as beetles and worms.

EARWIGS

These are yellow-brown insects measuring ¾in (2cm) long and easily recognized by the pair of pincers that protrude from the front of their heads. Earwigs are voracious eaters, decimating flowers, buds and foliage. They

hide during the day and feed at night. By placing an inverted flowerpot, loosely stuffed with straw, onto a cane near to the clematis plants, you will create a daytime shelter for them from which they can be removed and disposed of. Heavy infestations, however, may need spraying at dusk with pirimiphos-methyl or biferthrin.

APHIDS

Aphids are sometimes attracted to young plants. Fortunately there are a number of insecticides available to control them. Pirimicard is both selective and systemic, thus leaving animals, birds and beneficial insects unharmed. Many birds and insects feed on aphids and by attracting these friendly predators to your garden you may alleviate or at least minimize the need for chemical control.

VINE WEEVIL

The adult vine weevil, a greyish-black coloured beetle which is ⅜in (9mm) long, has a short snout and antennae and, like the earwig, feeds nightly on foliage. Their presence can be identified by notches appearing on leaf margins, often near the base of the plant. Control is difficult. They do not appear to be attracted like the earwig to a home of straw in an inverted pot, preferring instead to hide nearer ground level in plant debris, and are quite resistant to pesticides. The removal of dead and rotting plant growth is probably the best deterrent. Although the damaged leaves may look unsightly, the plant's growth should not be seriously affected.

Vine weevils cause infinitely more damage at the larvae stage. Adults deposit their eggs near to the roots of plants such as clematis, where they then develop into white plump larvae ½in (1cm) long that feed on stems underground. Their presence is not usually known until the plant becomes sick. Weevils consider plants in pots in the greenhouse to be the perfect nursery

ABOVE **This 'Gypsy Queen' is covered in the white powdery substance known as 'mildew'**

for egg deposits. Once again, good hygiene will help to deter the adult from finding a resting place. Watering container-grown plants with pathogenicnematodes Heterorhabditis megiolis in late summer should control the grubs before they grow large enough to cause serious damage.

CLEMATIS WILT

The major dread of the clematis grower is stem rot, commonly known as 'clematis wilt'. One day the plant looks bright and healthy, the next it begins to look droopy and sad. Within a week the leaves turn brown and then black, the flowers shrivel and die and to all intents and purposes the plant looks as if it completely dead. Research into the cause of clematis wilt has not yet been fully conclusive, but it suggests that a fungus called Phoma clematidina plays a major role. It tends to attack young green stems of plants in their early years. It works across the stem, cutting off the supply of sap to the plant.

The good news is that the plant below the affected area, which is often at a node close to ground level, is invariably unaffected. So the remedy is to cut off the stem below the affected node, continue with a good watering and feeding programme and with luck new shoots will soon appear. Sometimes only a single stem is affected and the others remain in good health.

Caution is required, however, before cutting down a plant so severely. Many a wilting clematis may only be doing so because it is thirsty. Water well; if it does not recover by the next day, stem rot may well be the cause and action will be required. Make sure all affected debris is burnt to prevent the disease spreading.

So what can be done to help avoid fungal stem rot? The most important factor is the gardener's ability to exercise patience. When planting any clematis, especially those that are more susceptible to the disease, follow the planting and pruning recommendations to encourage strong and plentiful stems. In some cases, a plant can be affected by fungal stem rot a number of times. Should this be the case, do not be in a hurry to abandon it. Follow the procedure of cutting down the affected stems, watering and feeding until the plant reaches maturity with some nice woody stems that are too hard for the fungus to attack.

Fungicides can be sprayed or watered into the surrounding soil in spring and again in autumn to help prevent stem rot, but it is recommended that various types are used throughout the season to deter the fungus from developing immunity.

Clematis growers have made great strides in developing new cultivars and hybrids that are resistant to stem rot, and eventually this disease may be a thing of the past. For now, for the gardener who wishes to avoid the risk, there is a wide choice of plants available with a proven history of resistance to disease, especially among the small-flowered varieties.

MILDEW

A white, powdery substance appears on the leaves, often attacking plants later in the season, causing the leaves to turn yellow and fall. It can completely disfigure the plant at a time when the flowers could still be giving a lovely display. The major cause of mildew is fungi thriving on plants in dry conditions. It is spread by wind and rain splashes. At the first sign of attack, immediately remove and burn the affected growth. If the condition persists, treat it with buprimate plustriforne, myclobutanil or perconazole. To help prevent mildew, ensure that the clematis is well watered and apply a good depth of mulching to preserve moisture during a time of drought and ensure a good airflow around the plant.

SECTION 2

CHAPTER 3

Spring clematis and their companions

Longer days of sunshine and gentle spring rain are perfect for the early-flowering clematis as they tumble over walls and fences, pergolas and archways, shrubs and trees, bringing a riot of colour to the spring garden. The tender shoots of the less hardy species and the young growth of cultivars and hybrids may be cut back during frosty nights. Many will recover well if the cold snap is not too prolonged. To help avoid disappointment, though, try to select clematis that are suited to your location and give the warmer spots in your garden to those species that are more vulnerable.

ABOVE *C. macropetala* seed heads complement a young wisteria growing on a house wall

ABOVE Pink *C. montana* adorns the walls of this picturesque cottage in mid-spring

CHOOSING SPRING-FLOWERING CLEMATIS

You may be fortunate enough to have space on a warm, sheltered wall for a rampant *armandii*, with its large, evergreen leaves and sweetly scented white flowers that appear in late winter. If, however, your climate is too harsh for such luxuries, you will have to wait a few more weeks before hardy *macropetala*, with her pretty, double, tutu-shaped flowers, arrives in early spring, joined by the equally hardy *alpina*, which is very similar in appearance and habit. If space is at a premium, these lovely early clematis are an excellent choice as they are quite easily contained.

Clematis montana needs a lot more space, but why not cover your shed, fence, or house with one and revel in the mass of white or pink flowers

ABOVE *C. montana* climbing over a doorway

ABOVE *C. montana* 'Marjorie' tumbles through the branches of *Prunus* 'Pink Perfection'

that waft their delicate scent on a warm day in mid-spring? After the blooms, you will be left with a luxuriant growth of attractive leaves.

Early, large-flowered hybrids also start appearing in mid-spring. Big and exotic, in a breathtaking range of colours, they are hard to resist. This is by far the largest clematis group and you will be spoilt for choice. You can use your trees, shrubs and roses as companions to a small collection.

Visit your local garden centre in late spring and you will probably see a good selection of container-grown plants in flower. To ensure that it will suit the home you have in mind for it, do not forget to read the label for details of the plant's eventual height and preferred location before you make a purchase.

ABOVE **The golden stamens of 'Gillian Blades' highlight the small flowers of *Corokia* 'Coppershine'**

EARLY SPRING
Evergreen clematis

In cold and dismal weather, it generally takes something very special to draw us outside – perhaps the glimpse of a flower that we would like to see more closely. If the flower emits a pleasant perfume, invariably we reach out to hold it close to receive the full impact and we are in touch with nature and our garden again. Clematis of the *cirrhosa* and *armandii* groups fulfil these requirements admirably with their pretty flowers that emit a gentle fragrance and their evergreen leaves. The only drawback is that they are not fully hardy and unable to withstand prolonged periods of frost.

The family of *C. cirrhosa* blooms from mid-autumn through to late winter, and has finely cut, evergreen leaves that are slightly bronzed

BELOW **The evergreen clematis 'Early Sensation' is one of the more recent introductions. When it has finished flowering, the lovely foliage will grace this simple wire-netting fence**

underneath. The flowers are cream, open cup-shaped, with some varieties having red flecks. The *C. armandii* group has larger and thicker dark green, glossy leaves that are a most attractive light bronze when young. The sweetly scented white, saucer-shaped flowers are borne in late winter and early spring. *C. armandii* makes an impressive sight when grown to its full potential, as it can reach 16½ft (5m) quite easily when content in its environment. Unfortunately, if caught by extreme cold and frost, it does tend to

droop and look sorry for itself. It seems to appreciate the company of other wall shrubs, such as ceanothus or quince, on to which it can wrap its tendrils securely and thus protect its large leaves from excessive wind damage.

Pruning evergreen clematis is not essential, but if you wish to keep them in check – because they are quite rampant – do so immediately after they have finished flowering, so that they have the opportunity to grow new stems for next year's flowers.

Companions for evergreen clematis

If you can provide a warm, sheltered wall, lovely partnerships can be formed between evergreen clematis and other frost-tender trees and shrubs. Acacia (mimosa), native to warm, temperate regions of the globe, is frost tender and can only be grown outdoors in mild climate zones. Of the acacia varieties, *baileyana* is a small, graceful tree of 16½ft (5m), *dealbata* is a larger tree reaching 33ft (10m) or more, and *podalyriifolia* is a medium-sized shrub and a more manageable size for a small garden, although its leaves are not quite as attractive. Mimosa's small, yellow, sweetly scented flowers, which are borne in racemes or panicles, look quite spectacular in late winter/early spring, especially when partnered with evergreen *C. indivisa*, whose pure white flowers and yellow stamens harmonize beautifully with the mimosa blossoms. Mimosa and *indivisa* are both ideal conservatory plants, where their fragrances will combine to create a heady perfume. When planting inside, use a very large container filled with a neutral or acid, loam-based potting compost, water freely during the growing season and apply a balanced liquid fertilizer monthly. Outdoor planting requires an acid or neutral soil against a sunny, south-facing wall.

Pittosporum is another genus of frost-tender shrubs and trees. The variety *tenuifolium*, with its wavy-margined, glossy, evergreen leaves, can withstand a short period below 32°F (0°C).

ABOVE Pittosporum, an attractive evergreen shrub, makes an ideal companion for early-flowering, evergreen *Clematis foresti*, seen here at RHS Rosemoor, Devon, south-west England

This lovely evergreen shrub, which bears dark red, bell-shaped flowers in late spring, followed by black berries, is an ideal host for clematis at any time of the year. For early spring, *C. forsteri*, with its pretty green-white flowers and evergreen leaves, makes an excellent companion. Both pittosporum and clematis enjoy fertile, moist, but well-drained, soil and full sun. A vigorous grower like *C. forsteri* will need space, but when grown over a shrub, such as pittosporum, it can also be allowed to tumble through other structural plants such as dwarf and small-growing conifers.

Clematis breeders fully appreciate the advantages of the evergreen group and one may wonder why people are not busy breeding stronger, more frost-tolerant strains. The answer is simply that they are very difficult to propagate, especially those that belong to the *armandii* group.

MID-SPRING
Macropetala and *alpina*

If your garden is too cold for evergreen clematis and a large conservatory is not at your disposal, you may have to wait until early spring for your first clematis show. *C. macropetala* and *C. alpina*, with their beautiful purple, lilac or pink, bell-shaped flowers, are well worth waiting for. Both groups are easy to care for and resistant to

LEFT **Pittosporum 'Sandersii' hosts large, early hybrid *C.* 'Proteus' which blooms in late spring**

BELOW **Clematis of the *alpina* type make good companions for camellias. Here they are seen in flower together; later, the seed heads will become a feature**

ABOVE The blooms of a pale pink *macropetala* will soon open and have the glossy leaves of *Camellia* 'E. G. Waterhouse' as their setting

pests and diseases. They are hardy too, and will withstand even the worst spring weather, looking lovely as they scramble through host plants.

Companions for *macropetala* and *alpina*

There are many garden plants that will virtually provide year-round interest. The small selection shown here may encourage you to use one or two of your feature shrubs and trees as companions to the dainty little bells of these early-flowering clematis.

Shrub hosts

Berberis thunbergii atropurpurea is a medium-sized, dense, rounded shrub with arching branches, bearing small, pale yellow flowers in mid-spring. The reddish-purple foliage is its main attraction, especially when it turns bright red in the autumn. This hardy shrub will tolerate almost any soil conditions and also partial shade. Established plants need about one-quarter of their shoots cut to the base annually after flowering to promote new growth. I suggest that you wear gloves, because the thorns on the stems can be quite sharp. A deep purple *alpina* such as 'Frances Rivis' will look stunning among the purple-red leaves.

Evergreen shrubs play an important role in the seasonal structure of the garden, and there is one that may be considered to be more beneficial to

ABOVE *C. alpina* 'Pink Flamingo' offset by the golden-green leaves of an evergreen

the clematis grower than any other, and that is camellia. Its beautiful flowers are on show in winter and early spring when so little colour is available, and its glossy leaves provide the perfect foil for a wide range of clematis throughout the year.

Camellias prefers acid soil and to be planted away from the early morning sun, which can scorch its buds and flowers. Feed it with a balanced liquid fertilizer in mid-spring and again, if necessary, in early autumn. Apply a deep mulching of acid leaf mould or shredded bark. When given these favourable conditions, camellias are hardy shrubs; they grow 3¼–29½ft (1–9m) tall, depending upon the variety. Remember that clematis will require a more intensive feeding programme than the camellia if these two plants are grown together. A feeding tube inserted close to the clematis roots will make this easier to perform.

Choisya ternata (the Mexican orange blossom) is a valuable shrub for year-round interest. The sweet-scented white flowers are borne in late spring and again in late summer

ABOVE **After Camellia has flowered, the glossy leaves provide a perfect setting for early hybrid 'Lasurstern' in late spring**

ABOVE *Euonymus fortunei* 'Silver Queen' has attractive variegated leaves all year round

RIGHT 'Pink Flamingo' is a beautiful *alpina* to grow with *Euonymus fortunei* 'Silver Queen'

and autumn. The aromatic evergreen leaves make a perfect foil for *C. alpina* or *C. macropetala*. Take your pick from those that are available to create a striking partnership. You should grow choisya in fertile, well-drained soil, preferably in full sun.

Euonymus fortunei 'Silver Queen' is another hardy, medium-sized shrub and grows to 8ft (2.5m). It is attractive all year round with its white-margined, evergreen leaves, the margins of which tint pink later. The greenish-white flowers, borne in spring, are rather insignificant and lend themselves to a partnership with the far

ABOVE **A superb golden conifer provides a glowing backcloth for *C. alpina* 'Ruby'**

RIGHT ***C. alpina* 'Frances Rivis' is a good choice for a pergola**

superior flower of a pink *alpina* or *macropetala*. To enhance the variegation, 'Silver Queen' should be grown in full sun. Plant the clematis on the shady side to protect its roots; the flowers will soon find their way to the sun. 'Silver Queen' can also be grown as a wall shrub where she will climb to 19½ft (6m). Both the shrub and the clematis will live happily without pruning, apart from what is required to keep them tidy and within limits, of course. If the clematis becomes too entangled you can cut it back, quite low down, and let it start again with new young stems. However, don't be too enthusiastic with the secateurs if the clematis is mature with very woody stems because the shock may be too much for it; it is therefore better to tackle the job over a couple of seasons.

Conifer companions

It is hard to beat a golden conifer for winter and spring interest. The size of your garden will determine the choice. *Cupressus macrocapa* 'Goldcrest' is a lovely conical shape and grows quickly to 16½ft (5m). It is good for a smaller garden and the foliage is a rich golden-yellow.

Cedrus deodara 'Aurea' grows to a similar height but it is slow growing with graceful, golden-yellow, pendant branches. *Chamaecyparis obtusa* 'Tetragona Aurea' is more of a bronze colour than yellow, especially when grown in full sun, but with an eventual spread of 33ft (10m) it is really only suitable for a large garden. The beautiful golden leaves of conifers make a superb background for both *alpina* and *macropetala* clematis.

Other supports

Macropetala and *alpina* are also ideal for growing on a fence, pergola or tripod, because

ABOVE *C.* 'Lady Northcliffe', a mid-season hybrid that is ideal for growing on a tripod, with a pink *macropetala* as its companion

although they produce a mass of flowers they are not as rampant as the late spring *montana* family. As the sepals die and fall, lovely seed heads remain to adorn the attractive foliage for many weeks. Towards the end of the summer, some varieties produce a light, second flush of flowers.

A tripod set into a border and planted with *macropetala* or *alpina*, together with a mid-season hybrid, will bring many months of colour.

The dainty bells of the early variety will be a picture in early and mid-spring, and the attractive leaves and seed heads will provide a pleasant setting for the large flowers of the hybrid during the summer, when it may be joined by a few heads of the early bells having their second flush.

Tripods are an ideal way to bring height to the garden. Small shrubs or perennials planted around the base will help to shade the clematis

evergreen shrub such as *Daphne laureola*, which grows to 3¼ft (1m) high and has a 5ft (1.5m) spread. The glossy evergreen leaves provide year-round interest and the clusters of slightly fragrant yellow-green flowers in early spring are followed by black fruits.

- *C. macropetala* 'Markhams Pink' planted with *C.* 'Lady Northcliffe' (deep blue). A group of *Erica carnea* 'Springwood Pink' would be a good choice for base planting. The pretty pale pink flowers bloom in early spring and deepen with age. Being evergreen, this small, trailing shrub will provide year-round interest and shade for the clematis roots. This variety of heather will withstand mildly alkaline soil.

Both of the above combinations can be planted in sun or partial shade.

- *C. macropetala* (the original lavender-blue species) with *C.* 'Guernsey Cream' is a combination best planted in a shady border to protect 'Guernsey Cream's' delicate colour. An ideal base plant is *Asarum*

ABOVE *C.* 'Guernsey Cream' should be planted in the shade to protect its delicate colour

roots and there is the opportunity to create some very pleasing combinations. You can take your pick of the *macropetala* or *alpina* varieties because they are all quite compact in size. Mid-season hybrids can be fairly rampant growers, so choose one of the smaller varieties. Here are a few suggested pairings:

- *C. alpina* 'Frankie' (mid-blue) planted with *C.* 'Gillian Blades' (white with golden stamens). Shade the roots with a small

ABOVE *C. montana* 'Pictons Variety' beautifully supported by a conifer's sweeping branches

europaeum, an evergreen creeping perennial with kidney-shaped, glossy, dark green leaves, which also enjoys a shady location. The purple flowers in spring are of very little significance, as the attractive leaves mostly hide them. This plant will positively thrive in humus-rich, moist, but well-drained soil, which is preferably acid or neutral.

- *Macropetala* and *alpina* types are ideal for growing in a container. Once they have flowered, their pretty leaves can provide background height for surrounding pots filled with colourful flowers.

The advantage of growing *macropetala* and *alpina* through other climbers is that it enables them to reach a height which allows us to look up into their bells and admire the beauty of their stamens and anthers. The twisted, hardwood stems of wisteria make an ideal support; clematis usually flowers a little earlier, but the partnership of clematis flowers and wisteria racemes as they form is most attractive and the clematis seed heads look lovely when the wisteria is in full bloom. The clematis will not grow to more than about 10ft (3m), so it will only ramble along the lower branches of the wisteria. There is more about wisteria on pages 84–5.

A climbing rose can be used to support *macropetala* or *alpina*; the clematis flowers will add interest before the rose blooms and their silvery seed heads will be an added attraction later, a glistening framework to enhance the rose's beauty.

These charming early clematis are so easy to care for and such a delight to see that they really are a must for even the smallest garden.

LATE SPRING
Montana

The massed blooms of *Clematis montana* in late spring will cheer even the greyest day, and when viewed against a bright blue sky they really are magnificent. *Montana* is a vigorous species and needs a lot of space. When grown through a tree it can spread to its heart's content and the sky becomes its backdrop.

The rampant growth of *montana* will swamp all but the very largest of shrubs; it is preferable therefore to grow them alone on walls or fences at the back of a border or on house walls.

ABOVE **The blue skies of spring provide the perfect backdrop for *C. montana* as it clambers through a tree**

BELOW **White *C. montana* clothing a large wall**

ABOVE *C. montana* blooms to great effect on a pergola

RIGHT Clematis breeders continue to produce stunning new hybrids, such as this one named 'Caroline'

If you are seeking to create a shady arbour under a pergola, take your choice from the beautiful range of *montana* varieties. In mid- to late spring, sweetly scented flowers will surround you and for the remainder of the summer and into early autumn the attractive leaves will continue to provide a dense, lush covering.

Early, large-flowered cultivars

Clematis breeders have done a wonderful job in producing such an incredible range of early, large-flowered varieties. They flower during mid- to late spring, then take a break to recover their strength to flower again in late summer. The bright pink 'Nelly Moser' with her distinctive stripe is probably one of the most well known of

ABOVE 'Nelly Moser' has a second, lighter flush later in the summer. Here she is seen growing with 'Ville de Lyon'

LEFT 'Miss Bateman' was introduced in 1869. She is now one of the older members of this group

this group and she is seen in mid-spring gracing many a garden fence or porch. Nelly, like many of this group, is quite hardy and unless nipped by frost will produce an abundance of large, showy blooms from mid- through to late spring

Not all of the early hybrids are quite as hardy; a lot depends upon their parentage. With so much breeding having taken place since the first recorded cross-fertilization between *C. integrifolia* and *C. viticella* by Mr Henderson

ABOVE **C. x *eriostemon* 'Hendersonii', the earliest recorded cross-fertilized hybrid**

RIGHT **Soft and gentle *C.* 'Guernsey Cream'**

BELOW **Bright and vibrant *C.* 'Prince Philip'**

in 1835 – which produced *C. x eriostemon* 'Hendersonii' – parentage has now become quite a complex issue. When you buy one of these hybrids from a reputable nursery they will advise you of its susceptibility to wilt and the general sturdiness of the variety. It is not easy to generalize, however. One garden may be able to grow a type that is considered to be susceptible without a moment's setback, while in another it may die away and recover two or three times before it finally settles.

With so many clematis to choose from within this group and with such a variety of ways for them to be partnered with other plants, you can undoubtedly create a unique late-spring garden that will be colourful through to the summer.

CHOOSING COLOURS

The colour range is vast, so including clematis in a colour-coordinated scheme will be relatively easy. You may have to use other genus for true yellow in the border – the closest the early-flowering clematis can get to it is 'Wada's Primrose' – and a really true blue is hard to find, although 'Multi Blue' with its silver reverse has only the slightest tinge of purple. A spring border devoted to two or three colours can look very effective, and it is currently fashionable to coordinate pots and features into a tonal colour scheme. Fortunately, gardening does not have to follow fashion. More importantly, it is a wonderful way to express your own personality. Nature allows a riot of colours, such as purple, magenta and red, to live happily together, and if this projects your personality then go for it. The large-flowered clematis of spring and summer will help you to be creative.

Having already promoted 'Nelly Moser' as a bright and cheerful early hybrid to grow along the fence or around the porch, there are of course many other ways that this popular hybrid can be grown. If you can avoid continuous direct sunlight so much the better, for this will fade her bright pink sepals. When growing 'Nelly Moser' or any other clematis through a shrub, there are choices to be made. If the shrub is of a flowering variety, do you want to enjoy those flowers on their own or would they be enhanced by a clematis as a flowering companion? Much will depend upon the nature of the shrub's flowers. Azaleas, for instance, are often so dense and vivid that the addition of another flower would be quite overwhelming. On the other hand, some shrubs have small, quite insignificant flowers which clematis could help to highlight.

LEFT 'Nelly Moser' brings a splash of colour to a hydrangea before the shrub's own flowers appear

If you have decided that the clematis and shrub should not bloom together, then you need to consider which blooms first. For example, 'Nelly Moser's' early blooms will appear before *Hydrangea macrophylla* but after magnolia. Both shrubs make ideal hosts for this clematis and are enhanced by Nelly's presence.

BELOW **Magnolia provides a magnificent spring display**

CHOICE COMPANIONS

Hydrangea is a popular genus with 80 or more species, but it is the mop-head and lace-cap *macrophylla* varieties that are most commonly seen in gardens. *Paniculata*, with its white cone-shaped flowers, is becoming more widespread; so too is the climbing species *petorialis*, a vigorous climber bearing a mass of white flowers during summer, perfect for clothing a north-facing wall. Clematis can be successfully grown through most hydrangeas, although it may become a little buried in the verdant *petorialis* climber. Clematis will also enjoy the conditions that are best for hydrangeas: humus-rich, well-drained, fertile soil and protection from strong winds. If the pH balance of the soil is below 5.5, these acid conditions will produce blue hydrangea flowers; above this pH and the alkalinity will create pink flowers.

Magnolias require similar conditions to camellias. Unlike the latter, however, some varieties will tolerate alkaline soil. *M. x soulangeana* prefers acid or neutral conditions and has a number of offspring with flowers ranging from white to pink to deep purple, depending upon type. As beautiful as they are, they can only really be accommodated in a large garden as they can reach 23ft (7m) with a very wide spread.

M. stellata is a compact variety for the smaller garden and will grow in alkaline soil. Magnolia blossoms are so spectacular that it is a shame to detract from them; their attractive leaves, however, provide a perfect setting for a clematis that blooms a little later.

Experimenting with various plant and clematis combinations is a very rewarding challenge, and with an abundance of early, large-flowered

ABOVE RIGHT **The magnolia blooms have finished, leaving the stage empty for 'Nelly Moser'**

BELOW RIGHT **This purple hybrid has the choice of clambering up the tree or through the magnolia. Eventually it may do both**

clematis available and an almost endless list of attractive shrubs and climbers, late spring offers a myriad of choices. Here are just a few ideas using some old favourites and a few of the more unusual hosts.

The fruit of *Actinidia kolomikta*, a relative of *A. deliciosa*, the kiwi fruit plant, is not of edible quality, but as a garden climber it is far superior. The heart-shaped deciduous leaves are tinted purple when young and turn dark green with white and pink tips as they develop. The small, white flowers in late spring are rather insignificant. When grown to its full potential on a warm, sunny wall, in well-drained fertile soil, *A. kolomikta* can reach 16½ft (5m) or more,

ABOVE 'Asao' flowers in mid-spring and makes a perfect partner for *Actinidia kolomikta*

BELOW *Actinidia kolomikta*, a spectacular wall shrub with unusual-coloured leaves in spring

making an impressive sight with its green, pink and white leaves. The lovely deep pink *Clematis* 'Asao', which blooms in mid-spring, will enhance the overall effect. Neither require much pruning, just enough to keep them looking beautiful. 'Asao' forms unusual seed heads which can be used effectively in flower arrangements.

Ceanothus is another shrub that enjoys the support and protection of a wall, where it can make twice the height of those planted in an open and exposed site. The Californian lilac requires full sun to develop its mass of blue flowers which are borne in spring, summer or autumn, depending upon the variety. Although it is lime tolerant, the leaves will occasionally turn yellow with chlorosis and require a treatment of sequestered iron. An annual acid mulch may also help to alleviate this problem. Like many shrubs, ceanothus enjoys fertile, well-drained, friable soil. Pink clematis provides a lovely contrast to the blue ceanothus, but most of the pale pink varieties fade if located in full sunlight.

The stronger rose-pink of 'Dr Ruppel', with its paler margins and cerise stripes, is more able to withstand the sun's bleaching effect. This is another combination that needs little pruning.

When we think of salvia, the bright scarlet variety *splendens*, which we grow as an annual, usually comes to mind. However, this enormous genus of plants includes some charming and unusual shrub-type plants. *S. microphylla-grahamii*, for example, has attractive evergreen leaves and magenta-pink flowers over a long period. It does not grow very tall, only 3¼ft (1m), making it an ideal specimen shrub for the middle of a border. Although it can be cut back in severe weather, it is certainly not as tender as *splendens*, especially if it is protected from cold

ABOVE **Bring something different to the shrub border by growing** *Salvia microphylla* with *Clematis* 'Snow Queen'

ABOVE *C.* 'Margaret Hunt' has been trained against a high wall to mingle with *Ceanothus* 'Autumnal Blue'. The delicate pink may fade in direct sunlight

winds. *Clematis* 'Snow Queen', with her large, white, wavy-edged flowers, makes a good companion for this pretty shrub.

Cestrum 'Newellii' is larger; its vigorous, evergreen branches can grow to 10ft (3m). The tubular, crimson flowers are followed by purple-red berries. For a vibrant partnership, pair it with *Clematis* 'Corona'. They can be planted in full sun or partial shade in rich, friable, free-draining soil. 'Newellii' will benefit from the protection of a wall, although it can be grown free-standing in a sheltered bed. Both plants will need only minimal pruning.

Robinia pseudoacacia 'Frisia' is a tree that is frequently seen in gardens; it is popular because of its beautiful golden-yellow foliage. Sadly its shrub relative, *Robinia hispida*, is rarely seen, although its leaves are equally as lovely and the

deep rose-pink racemes that bloom from late spring through to summer really are a spectacle. It is quite a trouble-free plant and fully hardy, not too fussy about soil, although it prefers moist, well-drained conditions. Like clematis, it does not tolerate too much wind, but on the whole it is an easy shrub and it is a mystery why it is not more popular. Maybe it is because of its size; with a height and spread of 10ft (3m), perhaps it is a little big for the average garden. If you have the space, just imagine that huge shrub covered in large racemes of attractive pink flowers surrounded by the beautiful leaves. Add a hybrid clematis of your choice and you will create quite a picture.

Early-flowering clematis hybrids need little pruning, making them ideal partners for a small tree. Choose one of the taller-growing varieties

ABOVE *Cestrum* 'Newellii' and *Clematis* 'Corona', two vibrant colours together

ABOVE *Robinia hispida* and an early hybrid clematis make a wonderful late-spring partnership

ABOVE RIGHT A pear tree makes a productive host for 'Nelly Moser'. You can enjoy the clematis in spring and the fruit later

RIGHT A few twigs have been inserted into the ground to give *C.* Guernsey Cream some support as she makes effective and beautiful ground cover

if you want it to climb through the branches. Just two good choices would be *Clematis* 'Belle Nantaise', whose large, pale lavender-blue flowers will bloom from late spring to late summer, and rich red 'Ernest Markham', which can still be seen flowering into early autumn.

Because of their need for water and nourishment, clematis should not be planted directly into the lawn. Plant it into a nearby bed and train it up into the tree, or make a circle bed around the tree so it can be kept well nourished by the timely application of fertilizers and mulch.

Unlike the earlier, small clematis, whose stamens are only on view if we are able to look up under their bell-shaped sepals, the lovely centres of the large, saucer-shaped flowers of the hybrids are best seen straight on or from above. Clematis make very effective ground-cover plants, but growing them in this way unfortunately provides easy dining for slugs, snails and other pests, so you may have to take extra precautions. A group of low-growing, evergreen shrubs, such as *Hebe* 'Karl Teschner', lifts the clematis away from the ground. Alternatively, small twigs pushed into the soil will provide effective support.

Whatever you choose as their companions, a selection of early hybrid clematis will ensure that your garden is full of glorious colour as spring makes way for summer.

Timely tasks

- Winter and early spring is the time to review whether the structural planting in the garden is working well. At this time of year, in northern climates, the garden is mostly viewed from the comfort of the house, so it is pleasing if each vista presents an individual experience. Perhaps one window looks out on to a pond or small water feature where plants reflect in the water and birds come to drink. The eye may be drawn through another window to a tree, such as *Prunus serrula* (cherry), whose copper-coloured bark glistens in the spring sunshine, or the ghostly glow of Betula (silver birch) whose white branches and bark shine despite the cloud and gloom. Evergreen shrubs, a clump of hellebores (Christmas rose) and early spring bulbs all help to create eye-catching features.

- Late winter/early spring is the ideal time to prune clematis that need it, and the extra expense and effort you made to label your clematis with their pruning codes will be rewarded as you face your collection of bare, twisted stems that all appear to be the same. While these pruning codes are invaluable, there is no substitute for getting to know the pruning needs of the various clematis groups and thinking about what you would like each individual plant to achieve in its particular location.

- You may have an *orientalis* or a large-flowered mid-season hybrid that blooms continuously from late spring to late summer. With these varieties you have the choice of pruning hard, pruning partially or not at all.

ABOVE *C. cirrhosa* 'Wisley Cream' does not require pruning unless it becomes too rampant

Much will depend upon where they are growing. If they are on a tripod or in a container, you may wish to prune them quite hard. If, however, they are happily scrambling up a tree or large shrub they can either be left to get on with it or pruned partially to encourage flowers to form on the lower stems.

- Clematis need plenty of water at all times, so when it doesn't rain for a few days do remember your watering can. They will especially appreciate being fed during their growing season, but once they flower it is best to stop feeding in order to slow down the growing process. That way it will be possible for you to enjoy the flowers for a much longer period.

- If worms have not already completed the job, now is the time to fork in what remains of last year's mulch, together with a handful or two of bonemeal to act as a slow-release fertilizer. While the soil is still damp, apply a new good depth of mulch to help preserve moisture and provide a cool root run.

- Tie in the stems of climbing varieties before they go off track or they will wrap their tenacious tendrils where they are not welcome: prize tulips, wallflowers, the washing line – they do not mind as long as they feel secure. Handle them gently because their tender new stems can easily break. Snails and slugs love these tender shoots too and will decimate these stems as they emerge from the ground unless you do something about it.

- Spring is a particularly busy time for the gardener. You may feel a little daunted by the jobs that caring for clematis adds to your schedule, especially if gardening has to be squeezed in between the demands of children, a full-time job and indoor do-it-yourself projects. If you can allocate some time to these tasks, you will definitely reap the benefit of a succession of lovely clematis that can be enjoyed all the year round. If you really have very little time to spare, I suggest you go for *alpina*, *macropetala* and *montana*, which you will be able to enjoy during the spring; they are hardy and quite independent and, unless it is an exceptionally dry spring, they will forgive the neglect that may have a negative impact on the large hybrids.

A planting plan for green and white (with a hint of yellow)

The trellis at the back of this bed could screen unwanted visual intrusions such as a dustbin, washing line or a storage tank. Although the planting emphasis here is a fresh, light, spring display, the phormium and osmanthus provide structure for most of the year. If the spring bulbs are interspersed with summer-flowering bulbs, such as white lilies, the rose and the clematis will ensure that the green and white theme continues throughout the summer.

When preparing this border for planting, dig in plenty of humus-rich compost, because many of the plants selected for this planting plan require fertile, free-draining soil in order to flourish.

ABOVE **'Arctic Queen' flowers early to mid-spring and also in late summer**

ABOVE **Climbing rose 'Rive D'or' complements the creamy stamens of 'Arctic Queen'**

ABOVE *Phormium cookianum* **provides year-round interest**

1 *Clematis* 'Arctic Queen'. Large, fully double, white flowers, the outer sepals often tinged green. Blooms early to mid-spring and late summer. Grows to 8–10ft (2.5–3m). The creamy stamens complement the rose.

2 *Clematis flammula*. Small, white, star-shaped flowers with an almond scent. Blooms early summer to early autumn. Grows to 13ft (4m).

3 Climbing rose 'Rive D'or'.

4 *Phormium cookianum* 'Cream Delight'. Broad, arching, creamy-yellow leaves with narrow bands along the margins. Tubular, yellow-green flowers in upright panicles in summer. Height: 6½ft (2m). Spread: 10ft (3m).

5 *Camassia leichtlinii*. Long spires bearing star-shaped white flowers in summer. Soil must be kept moist. Height: 4½ft (1.3m). Spread: 4in (10cm).

6 *Osmanthus heterophyllus* 'Gulftide'. Dense, rounded shrub with holly-like leaves. Small, white, tubular flowers appear from the summer to the autumn, followed by very dark blue fruit. Although it can grow to 8ft (2.5m), it will tolerate hard pruning to keep its shape and size within the symmetry of this border design.

7 *Anemone blanda* 'White Splendour'. Clump-forming, tuberous perennial with large white flowers in spring.

8 *Erythronium californicum* 'White Beauty'. Bulbous perennial. Creamy-white flowers with recurved tepals, born on graceful stems. Prefers dappled shade and must be kept moist.

9 Galanthus (snowdrops) will bring a touch of brightness in winter/early spring.

10 Crocus. Any white variety. To follow on from the snowdrops.

11 Narcissus. Any white or pale yellow varieties or a mixture of both.

73

CHAPTER 4

Summer clematis and their companions

Clematis will enjoy the sunshine of summer but not hard baked, dried-out soil. If rain is not forthcoming for any extended period, the watering can will need to be put into use; the mulching you did earlier in the year will help to retain moisture and prevent casualties. The large bold blooms of cultivars and hybrids, dainty viticellas and herbaceous clematis scrambling through the borders can all be coordinated to complement your colour scheme or planted in vibrant contrast for a bold display during summer.

ABOVE A late, large-flowered 'Ville de Lyon' provides a bright, bold backcloth to the lime-green of a young choisya shrub; the blue hydrangea provides contrast and the colours are drawn together by a bright pink dahlia

ABOVE **The herbaceous *C. jouiniana* 'Praecox' and *Lathyrus grandiflorus* (everlasting sweet pea) make a rampant partnership as they tumble through the border together**

LEFT ***C. viticella* 'Margot Koster' clothes an old stone wall with an abundance of blooms**

CHOOSING SUMMER-FLOWERING CLEMATIS

The early-season, large-flowered clematis that commenced blooming in mid-spring are still bountiful in late spring, quickly followed by the late, large-flowered varieties. These are the true showpieces of summer, with their big, bold blooms demanding attention as they tumble through shrubs and roses, climb walls, archways and pergolas or make a beautiful backcloth to the colourful summer border.

Although they are a little less flamboyant than their large-flowered relatives, many clematis enthusiasts consider the *viticella* forms to be even more beautiful. They are vigorous and hardy, so whether you choose a variety with dainty bells or saucer-shaped flowers, you will enjoy an abundance of blooms from mid-summer through to mid-autumn.

Clematis of the herbaceous group are not seen nearly as frequently in gardens as those of the climbing species. It is a great pity, because they make lovely partners for roses, shrubs and summer flowers as they weave their way through the summer border.

Clematis planted in large containers make a wonderful display on the patio, but remember to water twice daily during any dry spells. Some exciting combinations can be produced, with vibrant colours to excite and stimulate or soft tones to soothe and relax. It is also a perfect opportunity to grow one of the more tender varieties in a container, as long as you are able to move the heavy soil-filled container into a frost-free environment during the winter.

During the latter part of the season *texensis*, *orientalis* and late species clematis join the summer collection. As a feature of the autumn scene they are included in the next chapter.

SUMMER COMPANIONS

As you stroll through a summer garden enjoying the heady scent of roses, the beauty of the flower border or a flowering shrub, pause here and there to consider how clematis could enhance the existing scene. Planting clematis in partnership with roses, shrubs and flowers can ensure a summer full of colour and interest.

ABOVE *C.* 'Rhapsody', a recent hybrid, bears beautiful indigo-blue flowers from late spring to late summer, which are shown to perfection with the salmon-pink flowers of bush rose 'Silver Jubilee'

ABOVE RIGHT The curled sepals of late-flowering 'Sealand Gem' bring colour and interest as the blooms of 'New Dawn' rose fade

ROSES

Clematis and roses make excellent partners, as their cultural needs are similar: they both enjoy well-drained fertile soil, good food and plenty to drink. Meet these needs and apply mulching each spring and they will live happily together, giving an abundance of colour for many years.

You have the choice of planting clematis to flower before, with or after the rose. However, in practise, there nearly always seems to be a

ABOVE *C.* 'Huldine' blooms continuously from late spring to late summer. Here it is partnered with rose 'Raymond Chenault'

LEFT *C.* 'Vyvyan Pennell' often bears double flowers in mid-spring, although this young bloom is not sure what it is. It blooms before the rose and again in late summer

BELOW *C.* 'Arctic Queen', *C.* 'The President' and *Rosa* 'Handel' on an old stone wall

period when they are in flower at the same time as each other, so it is important that you choose compatible colours.

As already mentioned, a climbing rose can be used to great effect to support clematis before the rose blooms, and there is a large selection of early-flowering varieties that bloom in mid- to late spring that would fulfil this purpose admirably.

When we want the rose and the clematis to flower together, we turn to what are known as the mid-season, large-flowered varieties. They flower from late spring through to late summer.

To enjoy the rose on its own and the clematis later, we can choose the clematis from the late, large-flowering cultivars – the *viticella*, *texensis* and *orientalis* forms – and the late species.

Repeat- or continuous-flowering roses usually have a period when their blooms are sparse, between the initial flush and their second display. Clematis selected to harmonize or contrast will ensure a colourful array all summer long.

On climbing roses, it is a good idea to train clematis both horizontally and vertically to encourage an even distribution of blooms. One climbing rose could play host to two clematis. An early, large-flowered hybrid will add colour before the rose comes into bloom and can be followed by a late-season variety. You may well

ABOVE Late-flowering *C.* 'Jackmanii' and 'Ville de Lyon' with climbing rose 'Handel' create a vibrant trio on a house wall

LEFT The rose is in bud and will soon join mid-season hybrid *C.* 'William Kennet'. Together they will provide a lovely display throughout the summer

BELOW *C.* 'Caroline', another recent introduction to the early hybrids, makes a lovely partner for Bourbon rose 'Mme. Isaac Pereire'

find that there is a period when all three are flowering together – either in a softly harmonious combination or a vibrant display of contrasts.

As the season progresses, the lower leaves of some clematis varieties may become brown. By planting clematis behind the rose, unsightly leaves can be well hidden and the rose will provide shade for the clematis roots. Shrub roses and rambling roses are particularly suitable for this purpose.

BELOW Herbaceous *C.* 'Durandii' will continue to flower long after rambling rose 'Dorothy Perkins' has finished

Climbing clematis have a tendency to overpower smaller roses, such as hybrid tea and bush roses, so choose instead from the non-twining herbaceous group of clematis (listed on pages 142–5), allowing them to meander informally through the border and wend their way through the roses.

The border plan shown on pages 80–1 demonstrates how three 'Chinatown' bush roses can be grown with early and late clematis and other plants – cistus, roscoea, elymus, campanula and gentiana – to provide a long season of harmonizing yellow and blue. A high wall, fence or trellis at the back of the border is required to support the climbing plants and create the 'backdrop'.

ABOVE **Rambling rose 'Françoise Juranville' and** *C. viticella* **'Purpurea Plena Elegans' blooming in perfect harmony. This is an old-fashioned partnership that works particularly well in any garden**

Many of the old shrub and rambling roses, such as 'Françoise Juranville' give a magnificent display in summer but unlike modern roses they rarely repeat flowering.

Clematis of the *viticella* group have an 'old-fashioned' appeal of their own and make good companions to these old roses. *Viticella* clematis begin to bloom in early summer, just as the rose starts to fade; they may share a short time together, so do choose complementary colours. When the rose has finished, the clematis will continue to flower for a few more weeks.

ABOVE **Climbing rose 'New Dawn' and 'Madame Grange' bloom happily together all summer**

RIGHT *C. viticella* **'Alba Luxurians' flowers from early to late summer. It is seen here with the splendid bush rose 'Josephine Bruce'**

Yellow and blue planting plan

ABOVE **Climbing rose 'Maigold'**

Blue shades of clematis and yellow roses feature in this bright summer border. For a long flowering season, the location should be south or west facing. Underplant with yellow and blue spring bulbs for a lovely spring display.

1 *Clematis macropetala*. Violet-blue, bell-shaped flowers. Early summer.

2 Climbing rose 'Maigold'. Bronze-yellow. Fragrant. Summer.

3 *Clematis* 'Perle d'Azur'. Azure-blue, open, bell-shaped flowers. Summer to autumn flowering.

4 *Clematis* 'Durandii'. Herbaceous. Non-twining. Deep indigo-blue with yellow anthers.

5 Bush rose 'Chinatown'. Double, yellow, scented blooms. Summer to autumn flowering.

6 *Cistus x corbarienses*. Evergreen, bushy, dense shrub. Masses of white flowers with central yellow blotches. Blooms during late spring and early summer.

7 *Roscoea cauteloides* 'Kew Beauty'. Pale yellow, orchid-like flowers; early summer blooms.

8 *Elymus magellanicus* (rye grass). Densely tufted; intense blue; mound-forming growth.

9 *Campanula* 'Chewtown Joy'. Carpet forming; purple-blue bells; all summer.

10 *Gentiana* 'Sino-ornata'. Semi-evergreen; deep blue, trumpet-shaped flowers; blooms from late summer to autumn.

ABOVE **Clematis hybrid 'Perle d'Azur'**

ABOVE *Clematis* **'Durandii' and bush rose 'Chinatown', a vibrant combination for summer**

ABOVE *C. viticella* 'Purpurea Plena Elegans' and *Tropaeolum peregrinum* (Canary creeper) make bright summer companions. The Canary creeper, an annual climber, is not frost hardy

BELOW *Clianthus puniceus* has exotic red flowers in spring

CLIMBERS AND WALL SHRUBS

By creating colour at eye level and above with climbers, a new dimension is introduced. Summer offers the greatest choice for climbers. Unfortunately, some of the best are frost tender and need to be treated as annuals in most parts of Britain and northern Europe and north America. *Cobaea scandens*, the delightful cup-and-saucer plant, is a typical example, along with *Thunbergia alata* (black-eyed Susan) and *Tropaeolum peregrinum* (Canary creeper). Plants can be brought along from seed in a greenhouse and planted outside alongside a clematis, when all danger of frost has past, to create an impressive summer show.

Clianthus puniceus, a climber that originates from New Zealand, has long, fern-like, dark green leaves, which offset the brilliant red flowers, reminiscent of lobsters' claws.

C. albus, the white version, is often flushed green. This plant may survive the winter in mild climate zones if planted against a warm, south-facing wall and protected by fleece during prolonged frost.

ABOVE **The leaves of clianthus provide a perfect frame for** *viticella* **'Margot Koster' from early to late summer**

ABOVE RIGHT **The beautiful passion flower can make a good companion for clematis, especially on a large pergola**

There are a few varieties of passiflora (passion flower) that will withstand a moderate amount of frost if they are planted in a warm, sheltered site and if the wood has ripened well throughout the summer. Being evergreen and rampant, they can provide a green covering on a large pergola throughout the winter months, or alternatively they can be used to clothe a wall or fence. When nipped by frost, the leaves tend to have a rather droopy appearance, but during the summer their beautiful and unusual flowers are quite spectacular.

Chaenomeles japonica (Japanese quince or simply 'Japonica') is fully hardy; it is not a climber, but an evergreen shrub that enjoys the support of a wall. Between the long spring flowering season and the autumn fruits that can

ABOVE *Chaenomeles japonica* **(Japanese quince) is easily trained around a window**

ABOVE *C.* 'Hagley Hybrid' creates a stunning summer display, but will fade if grown in full sun

ABOVE *C.* 'Jackmanii Alba' has been beautifully framed by pyracantha flowers

be used to make delicious jam, the shrub can serve as a willing host to a summer-flowering clematis such as 'Hagley Hybrid'. Quince is particularly useful for growing on a house wall because it lends itself to being trained under and around windows. It does not object to partial shade, which is ideal for this partnership because the delicate pink 'Hagley Hybrid' will fade if grown in full sun.

Some of the genus of evergreen pyracantha can play a similar role to that of the quince, because their framework of branches can also be trained around windows and doorways. They can be grown as a border shrub or up against a fence. Whatever site you choose, they provide a lovely framework for clematis to climb. Bright orange or red berries follow the clusters of creamy-white flowers borne in late spring.

One of the most breathtaking sights of early summer is that of wisteria in full bloom. The long racemes of purple, lavender or white need no distracting companions. Walking under a wisteria-clad pergola is one of the best ways to appreciate their beauty. You can plant clematis and roses as companions to flower after the wisteria for a long and colourful season. Bear in mind that a very solid structure will be needed to support so many strong-growing climbers together. An established wisteria requires pruning twice a year. In late summer remove all the unwanted growth and prune the remaining stems to 6in (15cm) of the main branch. Mid-winter is the time to reduce the stems to 4in (10cm), leaving only two or three buds.

Often, the only space available that is large enough to support a full-grown wisteria is a house wall, for it is not unusual for these plants to reach 29½ft (9m) or more. When the flowers begin to fade, the graceful branches and elegantly formed leaves will provide a delightful setting for clematis such as 'Jackmanii Rubra', which will flower for a long period.

ABOVE **A magnificent sight in early summer, wisteria covers the front of this old stone cottage**

ABOVE ***C.* 'Jackmanii Rubra' and wisteria make good companions for a pergola**

LEFT **The lingering remains of a wisteria are almost obscured by a collection of clematis and roses on the upright of this pergola. White rambling rose 'Seagull' and climbing rose 'Summer Wine' harmonize with *Clematis* 'Rouge Cardinal'**

ABOVE 'Lady Northcliff' flowers a little earlier than honeysuckle and will continue all summer long

There are approximately 180 species of lonicera, but not all of them are hardy or emit the wonderful perfume that we associate with common honeysuckle, or woodbine. Few things conjure up summer more effectively in our minds than a comfortable garden seat, a glass of cold lemonade, warm sun, blue skies, birds singing, bees buzzing and the scent of honeysuckle filling the air. If you want to provide a haven like this in your garden, site your seat to the east of the honeysuckle so that its perfume wafts over you on the prevailing westerly summer breezes.

Lonicera is a rampant grower and comes in evergreen, semi-evergreen and deciduous varieties, the latter usually having the strongest perfume. It can look equally as good climbing walls, fences and pergolas, and being of a similar climbing habit to clematis it clambers just as effectively over shrubs and up into trees. However its growth is denser and it can dominate smaller shrubs.

Honeysuckle and clematis climbing together can make an impressive display and once again clematis can extend the honeysuckle's season. A word of caution, however: if you place two strong-growing characters together, they may fight for dominance, so choose less-rampant varieties from both genera, and ensure they have a good deep root run and are well watered and fed. *Lonicera x americana* has strongly fragrant, creamy-yellow flowers flushed pink all summer long, while *L. periclymenum* 'Serotina' bears fragrant yellow-red flowers in early to mid-summer. Both of these plants will grow to approximately 13ft (4m). Choose a large-flowered clematis for a bold display or, alternatively, the slightly more subtle effect of a purple or wine-red *viticella*. A pergola can provide the perfect location for honeysuckle and clematis, with the honeysuckle climbing up one support, the clematis up another, and both intermingling where they meet at the top.

CLEMATIS AS A BACKCLOTH IN THE BORDER

Given the right location and setting, clematis can be used either singly or in pairs to create a stunning backcloth to a border. Many front gardens have a border that is adjacent to the house, and the house wall can be put to good effect in this way. Fences, trellises and garden walls are invaluable supports at the back of any border and they add another vital dimension.

ABOVE Early large hybrid 'Vyvyan Pennell' produces single blooms for its second show, providing height and interest at the back of this brightly coloured, late-summer border

BELOW Late, large hybrid 'Jackmanii', an old favourite of the author, provides a lovely backcloth to this colourful front garden border

CLEMATIS WITH SHRUBS AND TREES

Even when all of the garden walls and fences are covered there are still plenty of opportunities to grow clematis through shrubs and trees.

Clematis that require hard pruning make ideal companions for spring-flowering shrubs such as camellias, magnolias, rhododendrons and azaleas. Clematis climb their way through the shrubs during spring and early summer, but do not compete with the spring show. Later they come into their own and bring another season of flowering beauty.

If clematis is the 'Queen of Climbers', as she is fondly referred to, then camellia is without doubt her 'King'. You can hardly go wrong when choosing a clematis to grow against the lovely glossy leaves of a camellia. The only predicament is finding situations in the garden where the camellia blooms will not be scorched by the early morning sun.

There is an extensive range of azaleas and rhododendrons, but do not consider planting them in the border unless it is of acid soil. If your soil is neutral or alkaline, plant them instead in ericaceous compost in a container placed in a partially shaded spot on the patio, away from the morning sun and cold winds. This family of shrubs requires shallow planting and regular feeding. You should deadhead them after they have flowered to encourage leaf growth rather than the formation of seed. Enjoy the spring spectacle and, later, a show of your favourite summer-flowering clematis.

The medium-sized shrub physocarpus will grow 6½–10ft (2–3m) and loves moist, fertile, well-drained soil, preferably acid or neutral. The beautiful golden leaves provide a superb background for deep wine-red clematis.

There are many shrubs that will grow in either an acid or an alkaline soil. Two flowering, deciduous shrubs belonging to this category are

ABOVE *R.* 'Luteum' is one of the few rhododendrons with a perfume. Here it is planted in a half-barrel filled with ericaceous compost. Mid-season clematis 'Elsa Späth' will follow a little later

LEFT Golden-leaved physocarpus and wine-red *C. viticella* 'Kermesina' make a stunning partnership

ABOVE *Weigela* 'Looymansii Aurea', a lovely shrub to host a clematis

RIGHT The mauve-pink flowers of late hybrid 'Margaret Hunt' perfectly complement this lace-cap hydrangea

weigela and kolkwitzia. The difference is in their size. Weigela should be pruned after flowering and allowed to grow to a maximum of 5–6½ft (1.5–2m), whereas kolkwitzia, the beauty bush, can reach 8–10ft (2.5–3m) and pruning is not so imperative. Both these shrubs should be given space in the border so that you can enjoy their arching branches festooned with a mass of pink, bell-shaped flowers in late spring/early summer. Later, these graceful branches can support summer-flowering clematis, maybe a *viticella* for the smaller shrub and a large-flowered variety for the beauty bush, choosing colours to complement other plants within the border.

Syringa vulgaris, the common lilac, is a large shrub or small tree that will grow in any soil but thrives in chalk. It is a great favourite with gardeners and rightly so, with its lilac, purple or white panicles of flowers wafting the sweetest of scents. It is sad when their short season in late spring and early summer comes to an end so quickly. While clematis falls short on perfume, their magnificent flowers can bring life to an otherwise rather colourless shrub right through summer into early autumn.

In spring, hydrangea was shown supporting 'Nelly Moser' before the shrub's own flowers had formed. Hydrangeas and clematis look very attractive when they flower together, especially if the hydrangea is one of the lace-cap varieties.

ABOVE The pink flowers of late hybrid 'Comtesse de Bouchard' is an unusual choice as a companion for the *Hypericum* 'Jack Elliot', but demonstrates how experimenting with colour combinations can produce superb results

BELOW Early hybrid 'Carnaby' finds a good home in a cotoneaster tree

The strident yellow flowers of hypericum make it a difficult shrub to place in a border, but if you have a dull corner or want a bold focus, this is the shrub to choose. There are a large number of different varieties, ranging from dwarf species to large shrubs, and they are mostly easy to grow. A deep purple clematis makes a very good contrast to the bright yellow flowers.

Cotoneaster, a family of deciduous, semi-evergreen or evergreen shrubs and trees, is an excellent choice for any garden. They bear white or pink flowers in the spring/early summer and orange or red berries in autumn. Birds love the berries and a flock of redwings can virtually consume a whole tree or shrub on a cold winter's day. The prostrate, ground-cover varieties provide good support for small hybrids or *viticella* clematis; the larger evergreen shrubs are wonderful companions for any of the summer-flowering clematis. An early, large-flowered clematis would be a perfect choice for a cotoneaster tree because they both require very little pruning.

ABOVE *Clematis* 'Jackmanii' gracing a variegated shrub

RIGHT Large-flowered hybrid 'Victoria' extends the season for this lilac shrub

Winter and early spring are the seasons when evergreen shrubs are most valued, but they also make good hosts for clematis at any time of the year. Choose a deep-coloured clematis without stripes for the variegated varieties, such as eleagnus, or the combination may look too busy.

The larger shrubs of pittosporum, as described in the spring chapter, can play host to clematis all year if given a warm and protected location. Their glossy leaves will enhance almost any summer clematis, and they look particularly attractive if grown with a deep purple *viticella*.

ABOVE *C. viticella* 'Etoile Violette' finds its own way into this pittosporum, growing well within the protection of a south-facing wall at Marwood Gardens, Devon, south-west England

ABOVE RIGHT *Osmanthus heterophyllus* 'Aureovarecata' is the perfect host for *Clematis* 'Proteus'

BELOW Bright and bold, 'Ville de Lyon' takes over as the blooms of escallonia fade

Alternatively, the purple-leaved variety *P.* 'Tom Thumb' forms a low shrub 3¼ x 2ft (100 x 60cm); two or three planted together provide excellent low-level support for a clematis.

Ilex (holly), whether plain or variegated, is another fine evergreen companion. The clematis flowers are followed by bright holly berries. Choose a self-fertile variety or grow a male and a female together or the berries will not form.

Osmanthus heterophyllus looks very similar to holly and provides an equally lovely foil for summer clematis.

Escallonia is a family of small or medium-sized shrubs, bearing glossy evergreen leaves with pink, red or white flowers in spring or summer. Choose clematis to complement the escallonia flowers or to take over when they have finished.

CLEMATIS TRAILING THROUGH THE BORDER

Clematis allowed to grow horizontally at ground level can provide a wonderful splash of colour in the summer border. Unless you want the bed to be totally covered by the clematis, choose a variety that is not too rampant and select a colour that will enhance other plants in the border. The herbaceous, non-clinging varieties make ideal companions for small shrubs and perennial plants.

Another method is to train some clematis stems up a fence or tripod, allowing other stems to trail through the border. Two clematis together, such as a large hybrid and small *viticella*, given their own space in the border or allowed to tumble over low-growing shrubs will provide a mass of colour for many weeks.

CLEMATIS IN CONTAINERS

With a little forward planning, pots and containers on the patio or terrace can be ablaze with colour throughout the summer, and by incorporating clematis into the plan, colour can be enjoyed at eye level and above. It is essential to plant clematis in large containers and provide the right conditions for their cultivation, so do read the relevant section in Chapter 2 before embarking upon the project.

If your patio adjoins the house and there is no opportunity for you to create a bed, a large wooden container that measures approximately 25½ x 25½in (65 x 65cm) and 18in (45cm) deep can contain enough growing medium to

ABOVE *Clematis* 'Huldine' brightens this bed of pretty pink cranesbill geraniums

ABOVE The deep yellow stamens of herbaceous *Clematis* 'Durandii' complement the yellow hermerocallis (day lily) in this bright summer border

support a collection of plants that will provide interest throughout the seasons. Place the container against the house wall onto which trellis has been fixed and prepare it for planting as recommended. The plans shown overleaf show two ways in which a large container can be planted, but there are many other ways you can create your own special mini garden.

Planting plan based on a pale pink rose

You will need:
1 container, 24 x 22 x 18in (60 x 56 x 45cm)
1 climbing rose 'New Dawn'. Clusters of double, fragrant, pale pearl-pink flowers from summer to autumn. 10ft (3m)
1 Clematis 'Miss Bateman'. Single, large white flowers with deep pink anthers. Flowers mid- to late spring, occasionally in late summer. 6½ft (2m)
1 *C. viticella* 'Royal Velours'. Rich, purple-red with deep red anthers. Velvety blooms from early to late summer. 10ft (3m)
6 pink lilies
3 white busy lizzies
2 pink verbenas

In the autumn, remove the busy lizzies and the verbenas and replace them with standard and dwarf pink and white tulips for spring.

ABOVE **'Miss Bateman', a stunning clematis for a container**

ABOVE **C. viticella 'Royal Velours' has a velvety sheen**

ABOVE *Rosa* **'New Dawn', one of the most popular climbers**

Planting plan based on winter-flowering Jasmine

This planting plan is predominately yellow and blue for winter and spring, and pink, blue and silver for summer.

You will need:
1 container measurig 24 x 22 x 18in (60 x 56 x 45cm) deep
1 *Jasminum nudiflorum*. Deciduous climber. Yellow flowers in winter before the leaves form in spring
1 *Clematis* 'Multi Blue'. An interesting plant; the blue flowers, with silver reverse, are double, semi-double and single, sometimes all blooming together. Flowers mid- to late spring and late summer. 8ft (2.5m)
1 *Clematis* 'Minuet'. From the *viticella* family. Cream sepals edged with rosy-mauve

Underplant with:
2 *Senecio cineraria* 'Silver Dust'. Grown for its silver leaves to complement the silver reverse of 'Multi Blue'. Pinch out the flower buds as the yellow is strident and the flowers insignificant
Fill in with blue pansies and pink verbena to trail over the edges.

In autumn, remove the pansies and verbena and fill with yellow tulips, hyacinths and blue scilla for the spring.

ABOVE **Autumn sun enhances the purple hue of *C.* 'Multi Blue'**

ABOVE ***C. viticella* 'Minuet' is an ideal choice for a container**

Timely tasks

Clematis will be growing rapidly, so check those on fences, walls and pergolas to ensure they have plenty of places to wind their tendrils. Those growing over shrubs and trees usually find enough natural support, but occasionally, when they outgrow their companion or the wind blows them off course, they will clamber up a new host and you are left with the delicate task of redirecting them. As summer progresses, the demand for water usually increases and reservoirs face the challenge of coping with national demand. Rationing is often inevitable and the thick mulching you applied earlier in the year will help to retain moisture and keep the root run cool. A tube inserted at the time of planting will ensure the content of the watering reaches the roots, where it is most needed.

CHAPTER 5

Autumn to winter clematis and their companions

Autumn arrives, heralded by a slight nip in the air and shorter daylight hours. Summer bedding plants begin to look tired, but once they are cleared away, a well-planned autumn garden can be full of warm and vibrant colour. Trees and shrubs that are chosen for their autumnal display; chrysanthemum; dahlias; Michaelmas daisies; the rich, glowing colours of sedum loved by butterflies; clumps of autumn crocus and cyclamen – all are perfectly complemented by the late-flowering clematis discussed in this chapter.

ABOVE The abundant blooms of *viticella* 'Royal Velours' clothing a tree trunk play a significant role in the overall effect of this early autumn scene at Marwood Gardens, Devon, south-west England

CHOOSING AUTUMN- AND WINTER-FLOWERING CLEMATIS

During late summer and early autumn, the large clematis that bloomed in mid- to late spring will often produce a second flush of flowers, especially if they receive a light pruning after their first flowering and are well fed and watered. Perhaps because they expend so much energy the first time around, the second blooms of the double-flowered varieties are generally single. Many *viticella* types also continue to produce an abundance of flowers, enabling some of the summer partnerships to be enjoyed during late summer through to early autumn.

Late, large-flowered hybrids usually continue to produce their splendid blooms in late summer to early autumn, none more prolifically and reliably than 'Huldine' which looks just as attractive when viewed from the rear, because its sepals are flushed and veined with pink.

ABOVE *C. viticella* 'Royal Velours' bathed in early morning dew

ABOVE *C.* 'Huldine' flowers for a long season

ABOVE There are delicate pink veins on the rear of *C.* 'Huldine'

When planning clematis for the autumn garden, the glowing colours of the season are best expressed with the warm golden-yellow of the *orientalis* family and the earthy pink of *texensis*. There are many varieties in both groups that look glorious when grown through climbers, roses, shrubs and trees.

As autumn progresses into winter and the air temperature drops to freezing, water vapour turns to frost. Only the hardy, winter-flowering *cirrhosa* will withstand such cold conditions and

LEFT *C. texensis* 'Ladybird Johnson' and *Rosa* 'Santa Catalina' provide a warm, pink glow

BELOW *C. orientalis* 'Orange Peel' and shrub rose 'Graham Thomas' provide a golden autumn glow when grown together

then only for very short periods. However, if you are able to find a warm, sheltered wall, or a conservatory, you can enjoy the cream bells and fine, feathery foliage of *cirrhosa* all winter long. There is even a variety called 'Jingle Bells' that can reputedly be in full flower on Christmas day.

LATE SPECIES CLEMATIS

There are many small, late species clematis that will flower until early autumn. They are not so readily available from garden centres, so you may have to treat yourself to a visit to a specialist clematis nursery to find them. If there is not one nearby, a catalogue and a mail-order service is usually available.

If you refer to the list of late, small-flowered clematis on pages 148–52, you will see that there are a quite a number of these little beauties available in a wide range of colours, shapes and sizes to grow as specimen features or in partnership with autumn shrubs.

C. potanini is a vigorous grower, climbing to 16½ft (5m) and tolerant of most aspects. The mass of small, white, spreading flowers with their crown of yellow anthers makes a magnificent display against a large evergreen shrub such as *Ceanothus impressus* 'Pugets Blue'. This 10ft (3m) shrub with intense blue flowers will make an impressive show from mid- to late spring, leaving its verdant green leaves for the display of *potanini* later.

C. flammula has an unusual almond scent and a mass of small, white, star-shaped flowers from early summer to early autumn. It looks lovely when grown as a specimen plant or through an open shrub such as *Hamamelis* x *intermedia* 'Diane' whose leaves turn yellow and red in autumn and whose spidery, deep-red flowers appear on the bare branches from mid- to late winter.

C. rehderiana is another late species that should not be missed. Provide a sunny position to enjoy its large panicles of cowslip-like flowers with a perfume to match.

ABOVE *Clematis rehderiana* looks and smells like cowslips

Clematis belonging to the *cirrhosa* group are vigorous growers if given the right location and conditions. In southern regions of Britain and the warm climate zones of Europe and the USA they will often survive the winter and produce a mass of beautiful flowers. In less temperate zones, grow them in a large container placed in a frost-free, well-lit porch or conservatory.

ABOVE *C. alpina* 'Frances Rivis', with its fluffy heads, and orange rose hips provide some autumn beauty

SEED HEADS

As the sepals of clematis die and fall, the plant sets its seed in the next step towards reproduction. Clematis seeds are very cleverly formed. Attached to each one is a little tail which helps the seed to become airborne in the wind and then, once it has landed, anchors the seed to the earth. These little tails are what makes clematis seed heads so attractive, and each species and cultivar has its own unique design. Flower arrangers love to use the more intricately formed examples as part of their autumn displays. They can also be a very attractive garden feature as they glow in the autumn sunlight or capture the morning dew. Later they glisten with a coating of frost.

It is not only the *orientalis* family that bears attractive seed heads, spring-flowering *Clematis macropetala* and *alpina* are especially lovely;

ABOVE *C.* 'Asao' in late autumn. The sepals have died and the seed heads are forming

ABOVE The attractive seed heads of 'Bill McKenzie' glisten in the autumn sunlight

ABOVE 'Nelly Moser' seed head clothed in autumn dew

ABOVE **The beautifully formed seed head of** *macropetala*

their silver twirls turn into fluff as the seasons progress and they prepare to leave the parent plant and launch themselves into the unknown. Some of the large-flowered hybrids produce intricate shapes that look as though they have been woven; these are especially sought after by flower arrangers.

The berries of cotoneaster and pyracantha look almost as good as rose hips alongside clematis seed heads, and the glossy evergreen leaves of camellia once again prove to be the perfect setting, this time for the silver heads of *orientalis*. There are certainly many combinations for the gardener to choose from.

ABOVE Glossy camellia leaves once again provide a lovely backcloth, this time for the sparkling seed heads of *C. orientalis*

RIGHT The last, lingering flower of this dainty herbaceous clematis of the *integrifolia* family will soon form into another delightful seed head

AUTUMN COMPANIONS
ROSES

Modern roses, just like the early, large clematis cultivars, will often produce a second flush the during late summer and early autumn months. In favourable conditions both clematis and roses can give a good show into early winter.

Most of the clematis early hybrids have a rest for a few weeks following their main burst during mid- to late spring, but there are some that will flower continuously throughout summer and into early autumn.

'New Dawn' is another climbing rose that blooms on into autumn. The pale, pearly-pink, sweetly scented flowers will tolerate partial shade, and it looks particularly lovely when grown on a pillar. In the summer chapter, 'New Dawn' was shown partnered with clematis 'Sealand Gem' on a simple wooden screen constructed to hide a storage tank (see page 94). This gardener had the foresight to plant both 'Sealand Gem' and late species *triternata* with the rose, and now enjoys a summer and early autumn theme of soft pink.

Several shrub roses flower during early autumn and it is not difficult to select lovely partnerships. *Rosa* 'Boule de Neige', for

ABOVE *C. 'Marie Boisselot' makes a perfect companion for the climbing rose 'Compassion'*

ABOVE *Rose 'Compassion' with seed heads of 'Marie Boisselot'*

ABOVE *Rosa 'New Dawn' with C. triternata, one of the most popular climbers*

ABOVE **The dainty, warm and very beautiful** *Clematis* **'Princess Diana' is one of the most attractive of the** *texensis* **family and a fitting tribute**

ABOVE ***C. viticella* 'Etoile Violette' provides a mass of colour on this rose-clad pillar after the rose blooms have finished**

instance, an old-fashioned shrub rose, grows to 5ft (1.5m) and has fully double white flowers that emit a heady perfume. Partner it with deep pink *texensis* 'Princess Diana' and the 'Princess' will draw out the slightly pink tone of this charming white rose. *Texensis* varieties look especially lovely when they are growing through pink roses. Additionally, *Rosa* 'Graham Thomas', a shrub rose with rather lax, arching branches and a mass of golden-yellow, double blooms provides the perfect foil for *orientalis* 'Orange Peel'.

Not all of the roses last into the autumn and those that are without flowers can look quite bare and uninteresting, but not when they are clothed in late-flowering clematis. Britain's wild clematis, *vitalba*, displays a mass of fluffy heads during the autumn, making quite an impressive sight in hedgerows and the edges of woodland as it partners the scarlet hips of the wild dog rose. Cultivated roses and clematis can be grown together in the garden to create equally pleasing and even more impressive hip and seed head partnerships. There are varieties of *rugosa* and *moyesii* shrub roses that can play host to clematis and provide three glorious seasons of colour. When coupled with *macropetala* or *alpina*, the dainty clematis flowers adorn the rose during spring before the

summer display of vibrantly coloured rose blooms commence. The silvery clematis seed heads and the large red rose hips are the partnership's final display throughout the autumn.

SHRUBS AND CLIMBERS

When the blooms of spring shrubs are just a memory and the flowers of summer varieties are fading away, clematis can bring new life to autumn. The glossy leaves of camellia and escallonia serve as a lovely background for clematis of the *orientalis* family.

ABOVE **Abutilon and the seed head of 'Bill Mckenzie' glow in early autumn sunlight**

ABOVE *Rhododendron* 'Sesterianum', shown here bursting into spring flower, plays host to *C. texensis* 'Glauca Akebioides' which will flower later in the year

RIGHT *Abelia* x *grandiflora*, an autumn-flowering shrub

Rhododendrons and azaleas that appeared so spectacular in spring now take on an autumn tint to their leaves and provide a perfect setting for the soft pink tones of a *texensis* or the golden sheen of *orientalis*.

There are a few late-summer flowering shrubs whose blooms continue into autumn and who can form interesting partnerships with clematis. Abelia is a graceful shrub which will slowly reach 6½ft (2m), especially if protected by a sunny wall and planted in free-draining soil. *A. grandiflora* bears white flowers; the pink flush will be complemented by a deep pink *texensis*. Together they will bloom throughout mid-summer and early autumn.

Indigofera heterantha also needs a sheltered sunny spot and free-draining soil. The arching branches are bare of leaves until mid-spring or even late spring. The purple-pink, pea-like flower is formed in mid-summer. If this slightly delicate plant is damaged by frost, cut all of the stems down to ground level in spring and new shoots will soon appear. *Texensis* 'Gravetye Beauty'

ABOVE *C. texensis* 'Gravetye Beauty' complements a bold red and white dahlia

ABOVE *C.* 'Gravetye Beauty' and *Indigofera heterantha*

ABOVE RIGHT *Jasminum officinale* 'Aureum' provides a golden backcloth for *C. viticella* 'Polish Spirit'

RIGHT *C.* 'Polish Spirit' weaving through wisteria

BELOW RIGHT *C. viticella* 'Polish Spirit', grown horizontally to complement *Aster divaricatus*

with its upward-facing, tulip-shaped flowers makes an ideal colourful partner for *indigofera* throughout summer.

The evergreen family of hebe originates from New Zealand and some of the more popular varieties are quite hardy. They are easy to grow on any well-drained soil and do not require pruning. *H.* 'Midsummer Beauty' has lavender-coloured flowers that will complement a deep-purple *viticella* such as 'Elvan' or 'Etoile Violette'.

Viticella 'Polish Spirit' will often flower well into early autumn, making it a perfect choice for the autumn garden. The deep-purple blooms are shown to full advantage against the golden leaves of a shrub or climber.

The deep pink of the *texensis* group also looks effective when they tumble over variegated shrubs. Grown horizontally through the border they make ideal partners for dahlia and other autumn perennials.

'Bill Mackenzie' is one of the finest varieties of the *orientalis* group. The golden bells are larger than type and some of the flowers die, leaving their silvery seed heads behind, while new flowers are formed at the same time, creating a mass of gold and silver to shimmer in the autumn sunlight.

'Bill Mackenzie' is quite a rampant grower and if paired with other climbers or wall shrubs will need a large wall or fence for support. Abutilon is a tender shrub but some varieties, such as 'Kentish Belle' or 'Milleri' will withstand some frost if planted against a warm wall. Abutilon's flowers and 'Bill's' seed heads make a glorious pairing as they shimmer in the autumn sun.

ABOVE **'Bill Mackenzie' and a late-flowering honeysuckle can easily reach the roof when grown on a house wall**

ABOVE *C. orientalis* **'Bill Mackenzie' and** *viticella* **'Purpurea Plena Elegans' cover a summerhouse at RHS Rosemoor, Devon, south-west England**

Timely tasks

- The seasons merge in a very subtle way with much depending upon the climatic conditions of the region and general weather patterns. Sometimes an early autumn day can be warmer than one in mid-summer and a long warm autumn, especially if accompanied by drying winds, can lead to an extended season for the watering can or hose.
- When we emerge in the morning it is dew that indicates that the nights have started getting cooler. The water vapour in the air condenses, leaving the jewel-like droplets glistening in the early morning sun. Fortunately, most dormant clematis survive even the coldest of winters with their roots snug under the ground and their stems protected by a strong, woody coating. A thick mulch of compost or well-rotted manure around established clematis

applied before the onset of winter will not only help to protect roots, but will enable worms and winter rain to draw the mulch down to feed the soil in readiness for next spring's root growth. Make sure you keep the mulch away from the clematis stems to prevent them from rotting.
- Autumn is also a good month for planting clematis in many regions where the ground is still warm and plants will have a chance to become established and produce flowers the following year.
- If the lower leaves of clematis turn brown and die, they can be removed. However, it is often pests and diseases that are the biggest cause of disfigured clematis. Mildew can often ruin an otherwise beautiful plant; this disease is usually caused by dryness around the root system and lack of air circulation around the growth. Preventative measures are the best answer. (See pages 32–7 for guidance on the control of pests and diseases.)

'Bill Mackenzie' has been known to flower in May if left unpruned and is therefore an ideal candidate for partial pruning. This works well if it is to be grown through an apple, pear or plum tree, because the branches will be clothed in beautiful flowers for many weeks and the seed heads will add interest during the winter months.

Another good late-flowering climber is *Tropaeolum speciosum*. A native of Chile, the 'flame creeper' requires moist soil and, like clematis, flourishes when its roots are in the shade and its head is in the sunshine. The spectacular flame-red flowers in summer and early autumn are followed by blue fruits with red collars. Plant it against a warm, south-facing wall. It may be cut back in severe weather.

ABOVE 'Bill Mackenzie' enjoys this south-facing wall with Tropaeolum speciosum, the Chilean flame creeper

Planting plan for a raised corner bed

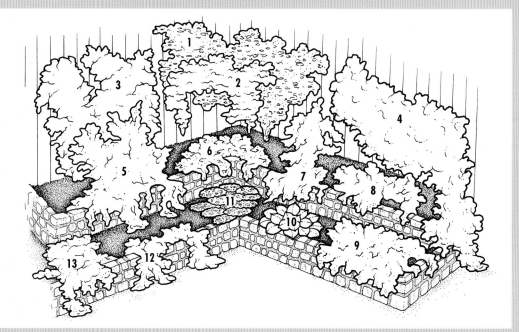

Boundary fences or walls can be used to good effect by building raised beds around a corner. This planting plan is aimed at warm and vibrant autumn colours with a splash of colour for spring. The beds will need to be built to a minimum depth of 18in (45cm). If it is adjacent to a fence, the back of the enclosure will need to be of brick or blocks, otherwise the weight of the soil will make the fence unstable and dampness will rot the wood.

While it is empty, dig the base soil and firm it by treading. Cover with an 3in (8cm) layer of coarse peat. Fill the enclosures with a mixture of four parts fibrous acid (lime-free) loam, one part sphagnum peat and one part coarse sand (lime-free). When the planting is complete, cover the surface with 1in (2.5cm) of sphagnum peat. The mulch will need to be topped up annually.

For the gardener with alkaline soil, raised beds provide a wonderful opportunity to grow lime-hating plants. However, if you do not want to go to the expense of filling the beds with an acid planting medium, then you can replace the rhododendrons and cassiope with alkaline-tolerant plants such as *Berberis thunbergii atropurpurea* 'Nana', *Hebe pinguifolia* 'Pagei' and *Hebe* 'Carl Teschner'.

Clematis is happy either to climb or tumble, and here they have the chance to do both. You may have to trim and train more than usual throughout the growing season or they will become entangled in one another and other plants as they tumble down over the beds. Parthenocissus (Virginia creeper) is very rampant and it is advisable to plant it further along the fence or wall and let it grow back towards the corner bed, as this will make it easier to control.

ABOVE *Solanum jasminoides* and *Clematis* 'Henryii' flower from summer to autumn

ABOVE *Clematis texensis* 'Duchess of Albany' brightens an autumn bed

ABOVE *Persicaria vacciniifolia* tumbles from a raised bed

1 *Solanum jasminoides* 'Album'. An ever-green or semi-evergreen climber with fragrant white flowers from summer through to autumn, followed by ovoid black fruits. This tender climber will need winter protection.

2 *Clematis* 'Henryi'. Large, creamy white sepals offset by chocolate-brown anthers. Can reach 10ft (3m) but will not mind being kept in check. A bright, glowing partnership with solanum from summer through to autumn.

3 *Clematis rehderiana*. Panicles of tubular, pale yellow flowers. Gentle, cowslip-like perfume. Mid-summer to late autumn. Will grow 6½–10ft (2–3m).

4 *Parthenocissus henryana*. White-veined green leaves which turn bright red in autumn. 33ft (10m) spread, but not nearly as rampant as some of the Virginia creepers. Will need to be kept in check, however, especially in a small garden. Prune back before it becomes entangled in the clematis.

5 *Clematis texensis* 'Duchess of Albany'. Tulip-shaped, deep pink flowers bloom between mid-summer and autumn.

6 *Rhododendron* 'Addy Wery'. Ever-green azalea with an abundance of funnel-shaped vermilion-red flowers in spring.

7 *Clematis viticella* 'Tentel'. Dark, rosy-pink flowers with frilled edges bloom between mid-summer and autumn.

8 *Rhododendron* 'Kure-no-yuki'. Evergreen. White flowers in spring. 3¼ft (1m).

9 *Persicaria vacciniiflora*. Creeping, semi-evergreen perennial; glossy mid-green leaves which turn red in autumn. Bell-shaped, deep pink flowers from summer to autumn.

10 *Hosta* 'Hadspen Blue'. Bold, heart-shaped, blue-grey leaves.

11 *Sedum spectabile* 'Brilliant'. The 'ice plant' loved by bees. Bright pink flowers. Summer to early autumn.

12 *Diascia* 'Salmon Supreme'. Mat-forming perennial with heart-shaped leaves and pale apricot flowers. Flowers from summer to autumn.

13 *Cassiope lycopodioides*. Evergreen, mat-forming shrub. Tubular, white, short-stemmed flowers. Late spring.

CHAPTER 6

Directory of clematis

There are over 250 known species of clematis, originating from both hemispheres. Many of these species were found growing in remote and wild regions, and we can thank the botanist explorers of the past few centuries for the wonderful range and variety of clematis that are now available. Whilst admiring the bravery of these adventurers, we must also recognize the valuable role played by amateur and professional clematis breeders internationally, who have cross-bred the species and produced so many beautiful cultivars and hybrids. The excitement remains today, with specialist growers and keen amateur gardeners striving to produce new and unusual plants.

With such a wide choice of clematis available and new varieties appearing on the market each year, it is virtually impossible to present a fully comprehensive list. This chapter is devoted to submitting as many species, hybrids and cultivars as possible to enable the reader to select clematis by season, colour, form and habit to suit his or her particular gardening needs. Finding new or different alternatives from your suppliers can be part of the fun of becoming a clematis collector.

ABOVE *Clematis* 'Special Occasion' a mid-season large-flowered cultivar

STRUCTURE, HABIT AND SHAPE

Clematis is a member of the Ranunculaceae (buttercup) family and the name is derived from the Greek word *klema* meaning 'vine branch'. You may have heard it pronounced in a couple of ways. Evidently the correct pronunciation is Klem-a-tis with the 'a' as in apple and without emphasis. In other words, it is not 'Klem-aye-tis' but 'Klematis'. This is not an important point, as it is such a beautiful genus of plants whichever way you say it, but it may be a little mystery solved for some readers.

Throughout you will come across the terms 'species', 'hybrids' and 'cultivars'. 'Species' indicates that the flowers and foliage are of the plant's original habit. If several species of one genus are cultivated together then they may 'hybridize', creating offspring that could well be similar to their parents or bear no resemblance at all. A cultivar, however, is an artificially raised plant and its characteristics can be maintained by propagation.

Clematis flowers appear in a variety of shapes and sizes from ½–¾in (1–2cm) up to 8in (20cm) across, or more.

The colour and formation of the stamens play a very important role, and it is often this feature that individualizes flowers of a similar structure and hue.

We are perhaps becoming a bit too technical when we state that clematis do not actually form petals (the corolla). The flowers are made by the sepals (the calyx) alone. On a rose we can see the combination of coloured petals and green sepals beneath. The sepals protect the bud and fold back as the flower opens to reveal the whorl of coloured petals. Clematis have a circle of sepals which, instead of being green, have developed into lovely colours and to all intents and purposes look just like petals.

To complicate matters even more, we often see clematis petals referred to as 'tepals'. This can only be very simply explained by the fact that in many genus of flowers the sepal and

ABOVE **Clematis are valued not only for their colours but also for the wide variety of flower shapes they offer**

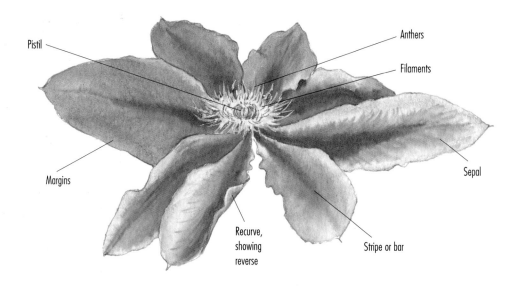

Pistil

Anthers

Filaments

Margins

Sepal

Recurve,
showing
reverse

Stripe or bar

The various parts of a typical clematis flower

Clematis cling to supports with their coiling tendrils

petals are identical and they both whorl around together; they are then collectively known as tepals. It is natural therefore that clematis petals could be referred to in this way. In this text they have been referred to as sepals, in order to provide continuity. This is a mere technicality, because whether we call them petals or sepals, they look like petals and that is how we tend to think of them.

Clematis that climb can only do so with the aid of a structure or host plant. As part of their leaf construction, they develop coiling tendrils that curl around any suitable means of support in their pathway.

In the wild, clematis naturally clamber over hedges and bushes and often climb high into trees. *C. vitalba*, the native clematis of Britain, often called old man's beard because of its fluffy seed heads, is a well-known sight at the edge of woods and forests and in hedgerows, where it makes a charming companion to the wild rose, particularly in autumn when the seed heads and orange rose hips are produced in abundance. Much can be learnt by observing the growth

ABOVE *C. alpina* 'Frances Rivis' blooms in spring and as a category 1 variety does not need to be pruned

and habit of wild clematis: they naturally plant their feet in the shade and climb vigorously over a host plant or tree to have their heads in the sun. This natural habit is what we have tried to emulate in some of the examples and ideas for garden planting shown in previous chapters.

The herbaceous clematis group does not have coiling tendrils and they can only scramble around and over other plants. Some varieties, however, will climb to 6½ft (2m) if given support.

PRUNING CATEGORIES

For cultivation purposes, clematis are presented in three categories:

Category 1 – *cirrhosa, armandii, alpina, macropetala* and *montana*. These varieties bloom in winter, spring and early summer, depending upon the type, and do not need to be pruned.

Category 2 – early/mid-season, large-flowered varieties which bloom in the late spring and early summer and require light pruning only.

Category 3 – *viticella, texensis, orientalis*, herbaceous, late, large-flowered, and late, small-flowered varieties which bloom from summer to autumn, most of which require hard pruning.

CATEGORY 1 CLEMATIS

C. alpina

Flowering season:	Early to mid-spring, some varieties having a second flush in summer
Flowers:	¾–2in (2–5cm) single, open, bell shaped
Aspect:	Any. Looks best when allowed to roam freely
Cultivation:	Hardy, follow recommended planting and feeding programme. Do not disturb roots when planting
Pruning:	Tidy only, because flowers are formed on previous year's growth. If necessary, prune lightly after flowering to contain growth. Severe pruning should be avoided when the plant is mature
Background:	*Alpina* species was introduced from mainland Europe at the end of the eighteenth century. Like *macropetala*, it is part of the Atragene group. There are a few selections of the species and a number of hybrids have been raised

Popular varieties:

alpina	Mid-blue with white stamens. Satin-like appearance. Approx. height: 6½–10ft (2–3m)
'Bluebird'	Pale-blue, large, frilly flowers
'Blue Dancer'	Silver-blue with slightly twisted sepals
'Blush Queen'	Strong pink with fading margins. Large-flowered, boldly presented
'Burford White'	White flowers

ABOVE *C. alpina* 'Pink Flamingo'

'Columbine'	Pale-blue
'Constance'	Pink-red. Semi-double. Occasional summer flowers
'Frances Rivis'	Sky-blue, lantern-shaped flowers
'Frankie'	Mid-blue with white stamens tipped in matching blue
'Jacqueline du Pré'	Rosy-mauve, edged in silvery-pink. A stunning variety
'Odorata'	Mid-blue. Sweetly scented
'Pink Flamingo'	Pale pink, veined darker pink. Occasional summer flowers
'Rosy Pagoda'	Pink with white edges. Flowers in profusion
'Ruby'	Rosy-red with off-white stamens. Occasional summer flowers
'White Columbine'	Pure white profusion of flowers with long, tapering sepals
'Willy'	Pale pink with red base

C. armandii

Flowering season:	Late winter to early spring
Flowers:	Saucer shaped
Aspect:	Warm, sunny wall in a mild-climate zone; alternatively, a conservatory or sheltered porch. Rampant growth; allow plenty of space
Cultivation:	Follow recommended planting and feeding programme
Pruning:	None required because flowers are formed on previous year's growth. If necessary, prune lightly after flowering to contain growth
Background:	Introduced from southern China in early part of the twentieth century. Some interesting varieties have since been bred from the species.
Popular varieties:	
armandii	Creamy-white. Large glossy leaves all year round. Sweetly scented. Approx. height: 19½ft (6m)
'Apple Blossom'	Pale pink buds opening to very pale. Rounded foliage tinged bronze. Apple-blossom fragrance. Approx. height: 19½ft (6m)

RIGHT *C. armandii* 'Apple Blossom'

'Bowl of Beauty'   White, bowl-shaped flowers. Large clusters. Dark foliage. Approx. height: 19½ft (6m)

'Meyeniana'   Cream with rose-pink flush. Large foliage, sweet scent. A very rare form introduced from Hong Kong. Approx. height: 15ft (4.5m)

'Snowdrift'   Waxy-white. Heavily scented. Glossy green leaves all year round. Approx. height: 15ft (4.5m)

C. cirrhosa

Flowering season:	Mid-autumn to late winter
Flowers:	Open, bell-shaped flowers and attractive seed heads
Aspect:	Warm, sunny wall in a mild-climate zone. Alternatively, a conservatory or sheltered porch. Rampant growth; allow plenty of space
Cultivation:	Follow recommended planting and feeding programme
Pruning:	None required because flowers are formed on previous year's growth. If necessary, prune lightly after flowering to contain growth
Background:	Introduced from southern Europe during the latter part of the sixteenth century
Popular varieties:	
cirrhosa	Evergreen climber. Cream flowers, lightly speckled red inside. Fern-like foliage, bronze coloured in winter. Attractive seed heads. Citrus scent. Approx. height: 13ft (4m)

ABOVE **Evergreen 'Early Sensation' lives up to its name as it decorates a wire-netting fence**

ABOVE *C. cirrhosa* 'Wisley Cream' needs a warm, sheltered wall or a conservatory. It can flower from mid-autumn to late winter

var. *balaerica*	Deep cream with maroon spots inside. Slightly broader leaves, finely cut. Pointed sepals. Approx. height: 13ft (4m)
'Calycina'	Cream, speckled as species. Open cup-shaped flowers born singly or in clusters. Broader, light bronze leaves. Attractive seed heads. Approx. height: 13ft (4m)
'Early Sensation'	White with soft yellow stamens. Attractive green foliage. Prefers a sheltered south-westerly aspect. Approx. height: 13ft (4m)
'Freckles'	Cream with grey tinge. Heavily speckled wine-red. Leaves larger than species. Approx. height: 15ft (4.5m)
Indivisa	White mass of daisy-like flowers. Small leaves. Approx. height: 15ft (4.5m)
'Jingle Bells'	Cream buds opening to pure white flowers. Attractive dark green foliage. Approx. height: 16½ft (5m)
'Wisley Cream'	Cream with green tinge and slightly broader leaves. Approx. height: 15ft (4.5m)

C. macropetala

Flowering season:	Early to mid-spring with occasional second flush during summer to early autumn
Flowers:	2–4¾in (5–12cm), double in appearance, followed by attractive silver seed heads
Aspect:	Any. Very hardy variety. Can grow 6½–16½ft (2–5m) even on a north-facing wall. Like *alpina* and *montana*, this group is best left to roam with a natural look
Cultivation:	Follow recommended planting and feeding programme. Take care not to disturb the roots when planting
Pruning:	None required because flowers are formed on previous year's growth. If necessary, prune lightly after flowering to contain growth. Avoid severe pruning, especially when the plant is fully mature
Background:	*C. macropetala* species was introduced from China during the early nineteeth century. The original species is still one of the finest, with its lavender-blue flowers tinged mauve at the edge

ABOVE *C. macropetala* is a hardy species that can withstand the wintery conditions of a cold spring

ABOVE *C. macropetala* 'Markham's Pink', a dainty clematis for spring

Popular varieties:

macropetala	Lavender-blue, tinged mauve. Sepals have a felt-like texture. Approx. height: 6½–8ft (2–2.5m) (applies to all varieties)
'Albina Plena'	White. One of the newer varieties
'Ballet Skirt'	Pale pink. Slightly larger flowers, very full
'Blue Bird'	Lavender-blue. Very large flowers
'Lagoon'	Deep blue
'Maidwell Hall'	Navy-blue, often edged white. Semi-double bells
'Markham's Pink'	Clear bright pink. Full double appearance. Approx. height: 6½–8ft (2–2.5m) (applies to all varieties)
'Rosy O'Grady'	Rose-pink, veined in mauve. Long, pointed sepals
'Snowbird'	White. Full double, slightly curled sepals
'Vicky'	Pink with silvery margins. Finely cut foliage
'Westleton'	Mid-blue, cream inside. Flowers larger than type
'White Lady'	Pure white. Flowers in profusion
'White Swan'	Creamy-white. Twisted sepals

C. montana

Flowering season:	Mid- to late spring (unless stated otherwise)
Flowers:	Open, single, 2–4in (5–10cm), scented
Aspect:	Any (unless stated otherwise). Vigorous, requires plenty of space. Suitable for growing into trees, over buildings, walls and fences
Cultivation:	May not withstand long periods of frost; follow recommended planting and feeding programme
Pruning:	None required because flowers are formed on previous year's growth. If necessary, prune immediately after flowering to contain growth
Background:	*C. montana* species was originally introduced in the early part of the nineteenth century from the Himalayas, followed by other varieties from India and China. Many beautiful cultivars and hybrids have since been raised
Popular varieties:	
montana	White. Profusion of flowers. Approx. height: 19½–33ft (6–10m)
'Broughton Star'	Deep pink with cream stamens. Double flowers. Purple-bronze foliage. Approx. height: 16½–21ft (5–6.5m)
'Elizabeth'	Pink. Vanilla scent; sunny site for perfume. Approx. height: 19½–33ft (6–10m)
'Fragrant Spring'	Pink. Very sweetly scented. Attractive bronze foliage. Approx. height: 19½–33ft (6–10m)
'Freda'	Cherry-pink with cream stamens. Bronze foliage. Approx. height: 13–16½ft (4–5m)
'Grandiflora'	White with bright yellow anthers. Large flowers in profusion. Deep grey-green foliage. Approx. height: 19½–33ft (6–10m)

ABOVE **The bronze foliage of *C. montana* 'Broughton Star' complements the deep pink double flowers**

'Margaret Jones'	Pure white. Double flowers. Approx. height: 33ft (10m)
'Marjorie'	Salmon-pink with darker markings. Semi-double. Needs a sunny site to develop full colour. Approx. height: 33ft (10m)
'Mayleen'	Pink with wavy-edged sepals. Bronze foliage. Sweetly scented. Approx. height: 19½–33ft (6–10m)
'Peveril'	Pure white with yellow stamens. Flowers later than type – early summer; flowers on long stalks. Approx. height: 16½–19½ft (5–6m)
'Picton's Variety'	Deep rose-pink. Attractive bronze foliage. Approx. height: 16½ft (5m)
'Pink Perfection'	Deep pink flowers with deep red stems. Dark foliage. Approx. height: 19½–33ft (6–10m)
'Rubens'	Deep pink with gold stamens. One of the most widely grown of the *montana* group. Approx. height: 19½–33ft (6–10m)
'Superba'	Pink. Flowers larger than type. Approx. height: 19½–33ft (6–10m)
'Tetrarose'	Deep lilac-pink. Attractive bronze foliage. Delicate spicy scent. Approx. height: 19½ft (6m)
'Warwickshire Rose'	Deep pink. Unusual dark red foliage. Approx. height: 19½ft (6m)
'Wilsonii'	White with cream-yellow sepals which are twisted. Flowers later: late spring to early summer. Approx. height: 19½–33ft (6–10m)

ABOVE The sweetly scented *C. montana* 'Elizabeth'

123

CATEGORY 2 CLEMATIS

Early to mid-season, large-flowered cultivars

Flowering season:	Early varieties: mid- to late spring and late summer; mid-season varieties: late spring to late summer
Description:	Flowers are mostly saucer shaped, 4–8in (10–20cm), single, semi-double and fully double
Aspect:	Any (unless stated). Pale colours can fade in full sun. Late frosts can damage early top growth
Cultivation:	Follow recommended planting and feeding instructions outlined in Chapter 2. Carefully train the young shoots to grow horizontally as well as vertically or flowers will be all above eye level
Pruning:	Early varieties: light prune only, because flowers are formed on previous year's growth; mid-season varieties: optional light, hard or partial pruning, depending on the situation. Note: mid-season varieties are marked with abbreviation 'ms'
Background:	Most species were discovered by the end of the nineteenth century. Cross-breeding has resulted in many beautiful new varieties. Their large blooms can bring a spectacular early show to the garden with the added bonus of a second flush in the early autumn. Mid-season varieties bloom continuously from late spring
Popular varieties:	
'Alabast'	Cream with yellow anthers. Plant in semi-shade to protect colouring. Second flush of flowers in mid-summer. Approx. height: 8–10ft (2.5–3m)
'Alice Fisk'	Pale blue with brown stamens. Large flowers. Approx. height: 6½–8ft (2–2.5m)
'Allanah' (ms)	Ruby-red with brown stamens. Very large flowers late spring to late summer. Approx. height: 10–13ft (3–4m)
'Anna'	Silvery-pink with pale pink stripes. Plant in shade to protect delicate colouring. Approx. height: 6½–8ft (2–2.5m)
'Annabel' (ms)	Powder-blue with cream stamens. Flowers from late spring to late summer. Approx. height: 8–10ft (2.5–3m)
'Anna Louise'	Purple with bold red stripes. Very large flowers. Second flush can be as early as mid-summer. Approx. height: 6½–8ft (2–2.5m)
'Arctic Queen'	White, large, fully double flowers. Approx. height: 8–10ft (2.5–3m)
'Asagasumi'	Pearly-white flowers with pale lilac at the centre of the sepals and cream stamens. Plant in semi-shade to protect delicate colouring. Approx. height: 8–10ft (2.5–3m)
'Asao'	Deep pink with white bars. Another lovely variety from Japan. Approx. height: 6½–8ft (2–2.5m)
'Barbara Dibley'	Petunia-red with deeper stripes. Pointed sepals. Approx. height: 6½–8ft (2–2.5m)

ABOVE *C.* 'Barbara Jackman' has lovely cream stamens offset by dramatic carmine stripes

'Barbara Jackman'	Mauve-blue with carmine stripes and cream stamens. Named after the wife of Rowland Jackman, a famous breeder. Approx. height: 6½–8ft (2–2.5m)
'Beauty of Richmond' (ms)	Pale mauve with deep blue bars. Flowers late spring to late summer. Approx. height: 8–10ft (2.5–3m)
'Beauty of Worcester'	Deep blue with white centre. Large, fully double flowers, single in late summer. Approx. height: 6½–8ft (2–2.5m)
'Bees Jubilee'	Pale mauve-pink with deeper pink stripes. Good second flowering in late summer. Approx. height: 6½–8ft (2–2.5m)
'Belle Nantaise' (ms)	Pale lavender-blue with prominent cream stamens. Very large flowers during late spring to late summer. Approx. height: 10–13ft (3–4m)
'Belle of Woking'	Silver-lilac with yellow stamens. Heavy heads best supported by growing through shrubs. Approx. height: 6½–8ft (2–2.5m)
'Blue Gem'	Lavender-blue with deep blue veining. Overlapping sepals form a rounded flower. Approx. height: 8–10ft (2.5–3m)
'Blue Ravine'	Mauve-blue with deeper veining, contrasting purple and white stamens. Very free-flowering. Approx. height: 6½–8ft (2–2.5m)

ABOVE *C.* 'Charissima' has very large flowers and can be grown in sun or semi-shade

'Bracebridge Star'	Pale mauve with carmine stripes. Large, well-spaced sepals. Approx. height: 8–10ft (2.5–3m)
'Capitaine Thuilleaux'	Cream with bright pink stripes. Crimson anthers. Best grown in semi-shade. Approx. height: 8–10ft (2.5–3m)
'Carnaby'	Deep pink with pale edges. Compact and free-flowering, ideal for containers. Approx. height: 6½ft (2m)
'Caroline'	Soft pink. One of the new hybrids. Approx. height: 8–10ft (2.5–3m)
'Chalcedony'	Ice-blue with gold stamens. Fully double flowers early and late season. A dramatic show. Approx. height: 8–10ft (2.5–3m)
'Charissima'	Cerise-pink with deep pink stripes. Long, pointed sepals. Approx. height: 8–10ft (2.5–3m)
'Corona'	Crimson, edged in purple. A compact plant suitable for containers. Approx. height: 6½ft (2m)
'Countess of Lovelace'	Lilac-blue. Double flowers early, single later. Approx. height: 8–10ft (2.5–3m)
'Crimson King' (ms)	Crimson with white filaments and brown anthers. A long flowering season, late spring to late summer. Approx. height: 8–10ft (2.5–3m)
'Daniel Deronda'	Violet-blue with sepals fading to a very pale blue. Occasional semi-double early flowers, single later. Approx. height: 8–10ft (2.5–3m)
'Dawn'	Pearly-pink with prominent purple anthers. Plant in shade to protect delicate colouring. Approx. height: 8–10ft (2.5–3m)

'Dorothy Tolver'   Mauve-pink with yellow anthers. Occasionally semi-double. Approx. height: 10–13ft (3–4m)

'Dorothy Walton'   Mauve with pink-mauve mottling. Long, pointed sepals. Approx. height: 10–13ft (3–4m)

'Dr Ruppel'   Rose-pink with paler margins and cerise stripes. Strong-growing variety. Approx. height: 8–10ft (2.5–3m)

'Duchess of Edinburgh'   White with prominent golden stamens. Fully double flowers with unusual mottled white leaves below the flowers. Approx. height: 6½–8ft (2–2.5m)

'Duchess of Sutherland' (ms)   Carmine with cream stamens. Flowers late spring to late summer. Approx. height: 8–10ft (2.5–3m)

'Edith'   Creamy-white with maroon anthers. Very free-flowering during late spring to late summer. A good choice for containers. Approx. height: 6½–8ft (2–2.5m)

'Edomurasaki'   Deep purple with rich red stamens. Its name means old Edo (Tokyo) purple. Approx. height: 8–10ft (2.5–3m)

ABOVE *C. 'Duchess of Edinburgh', an early-flowering double with unusual leaves*

'Edouard Desfossé'	Pale blue with blue-mauve stripes and purple anthers. Compact and free-flowering. Ideal for containers. Approx. height: 6½ft (2m)
'Elsa Späth' (ms)	Violet-blue with red stamens. Flowers late spring to late summer. Approx. height: 6½–8ft (2–2.5m)
'Empress of India' (ms)	Mauve-red with bright red stripes. Large flowers late spring to late summer. Approx. height: 8–10ft (2.5–3m)
'Ernest Markham' (ms)	Rich red with golden stamens. Prune half of the stems hard to have flowers late spring to early autumn. Approx. height: 10–13ft (3–4m)
'Etoile de Malicorne'	Deep mauve with subtle paler mauve stripes. Grows well in any aspect. Approx. height: 8–10ft (2.5–3m)
'Etoile de Paris'	Violet-blue with deeper stripes. Large flowers with short, pointed sepals create a distinctive appearance. Approx. height: 6½–8ft (2–2.5m)
'Fair Rosamond' (ms)	Bluish-white tinged with pale pink bars. Lightly scented flowers late spring to late summer. Plant in semi-shade to prevent fading. Approx. height: 6½–8ft (2–2.5m)
'Fairy Queen' (ms)	Pale pink with deeper pink stripes. Flowers late spring to late summer. Semi-shade to prevent fading. Approx. height: 10–13ft (3–4m)
'Fireworks'	Purple with reddish-mauve stripes. Unusual kinked sepals. Approx. height: 8–10ft (2.5–3m)
'Fujimusume'	Bright sky-blue. Compact and free-flowering over a long period. Approx. height: 6½–8ft (2–2.5m)
'General Sikorski' (ms)	Mauve-blue, gold stamens. Large flowers have satin effect and do not fade; late spring to late summer. Approx. height: 8–10ft (2.5–3m)
'Gillian Blades'	White, initially tinged mauve, with golden-yellow stamens. Sepals have attractive wavy edges. Approx. height: 6½–8ft (2–2.5m)
'Gladys Picard' (ms)	White, tinged blue. Produces large flowers during late spring to late summer. Approx. height: 8–10ft (2.5–3m)
'Guernsey Cream'	Cream with green stripes on first opening. Plant in semi-shade to protect delicate colour. Approx. height: 8–10ft (2.5–3m)
'Haku Ookan'	Violet-purple with prominent creamy-white stamens. Compact. Approx. height: 6½–8ft (2–2.5m)
'Helen Cropper'	Pale pink with irregular deep pink markings. Large flowers. Approx. height: 6½–8ft (2–2.5m)
'Henryi' (ms)	Creamy-white with brown anthers. Large flowers late spring to late summer. Approx. height: 10–11½ft (3–3.5m)
'Herbert Johnson' (ms)	Reddish-purple with maroon anthers. Flowers late spring to late summer. Approx. height: 8–10ft (2.5–3m)
'H. F. Young'	Wedgwood-blue with cream stamens. Good choice for containers. Approx. height: 6½–8ft (2–2.5m)
'Hikarugenji'	Bright lavender-blue with golden stamens. Fully double. Approx. height: 6½–8ft (2–2.5m)
'Horn of Plenty'	Rosy-mauve with deep red centre. Large, attractive flowers. Approx. height: 8–10ft (2.5–3m)

ABOVE *C.* 'Ernest Markham' will flower for a very long period if only half of the stems are pruned

'Imperial'	Pale purple-pink fading to white at edges. Deep pink anthers. Large flowers; free-flowering. Approx. height: 8–10ft (2.5–3m)
'Ishobel'	White, initially tinged blue. Attractive wavy-edged sepals. Approx. height: 8–10ft (2.5–3m)
'Ivan Olsen'	Ice-blue large flowers, edged slightly deeper blue. Purple anthers. Approx. height: 8–10ft (2.5–3m)
'James Mason'	White with deep red anthers. Large flowers with attractive wavy edges. Approx. height: 6½–8ft (2–2.5m)
'Joan Picton'	Very pale lilac large flowers, edged in deeper lilac. Approx. height: 8–10ft (2.5–3m)

'John Paul II' (ms) — Cream with pale pink stripes and red stamens. Flowers late spring to late summer. Plant in semi-shade to protect delicate colour. Approx. height: 8–10ft (2.5–3m)

'John Warren' (ms) — Pale silvery-pink with deeper pink stripes. Plant in semi-shade to protect delicate colour. Flowers late spring to late summer. Approx. height: 8–10ft (2.5–3m)

Josephine ('Evijohill') — Cream flowers with deeper cream stamens. Approx. height: 8–10ft (2.5–3m)

'Kathleen Dunford' — Rosy-purple with golden stamens. Large semi-double flowers early, single later. Approx. height: 8–10ft (2.5–3m)

'Kathleen Wheeler' (ms) — Powdery mauve with cream-coloured stamens. Very large flowers from late spring through to late summer. Approx. height: 8–10ft (2.5–3m)

'Keith Richardson' — Crimson flowers with red stripes. It is a hybrid of 'Barbara Dibley' x 'Lincoln Star'. Approx. height: 8–10ft (2.5–3m)

'Ken Donson' — Deep blue flowers with golden stamens. It is a hybrid of 'Barbara Jackman' x 'Daniel Deronda'. Approx. height: 8–10ft (2.5–3m)

ABOVE 'Guernsey Cream', delicate and beautifully formed

ABOVE The attractive mid-blue flowers and yellow stamens of C. 'Lasurstern' has made it an understandably popular early-flowering hybrid

'King Edward VII' (ms)	Mauve-pink with red anthers. Very large flowers during late spring to late summer. Approx. height: 8–10ft (2.5–3m)
'King George V' (ms)	Very pale pink with bright pink stripes; late spring to late summer. A feature plant when well placed. Approx. height: 6½–8ft (2–2.5m)
'Kiri Te Kanawa'	Deep blue. Fully double flowers early and later. Approx. height: 6½–8ft (2–2.5m)
'Königskind'	Pale violet with deep purple anthers. Very free-flowering. Good choice for containers. Approx. height: 6½–8ft (2–2.5m)
'Lady Caroline Nevill' (ms)	Pale lavender-blue with white bars and red stamens. Semi-double flowers early, single later. Flowers late spring to late summer. Approx. height: 10–13ft (3–4m)
'Lady Londesborough'	Pale silvery-mauve. Plant in sheltered position and semi-shade to prevent fading. Approx. height: 6½–8ft (2–2.5m)
'Lady Northcliffe' (ms)	Deep blue with cream stamens. Flowers late spring to late summer. Approx. height: 6½–8ft (2–2.5m)
'Lasurstern'	Mid-blue with yellow stamens. Large flowers. Approx. height: 10–13ft (3–4m)

131

ABOVE *C. lilacina floribunda* has unusual twisted sepals giving it quite a quirky character

'Lawsoniana'	Pale blue with rosy tint; beige anthers. Very large flowers. Approx. height: 8–10ft (2.5–3m)
'Lemon Chiffon'	Creamy, almost yellow on first opening. Yellow stamens. Plant in semi-shade to protect colouring. Approx. height: 6½–8ft (2–2.5m)
'Liberation'	Deep cerise-pink, fading at edges to pale pink, with cream prominent stamens. Approx. height: 8–10ft (2.5–3m)
lilacina floribunda	Deep lilac-purple with reddish-brown anthers. Unusual twisted sepals. Approx. height: 8–10ft (2.5–3m)
'Lilac Time'	Wisteria-blue, flecked with darker blue. Semi-double flowers early, single later. Approx. height: 6½–8ft (2–2.5m)

'Lincoln Star'	Raspberry-pink with red anthers. Approx. height: 8–10ft (2.5–3m)
'Lord Nevill'	Bright royal blue. Prefers a southerly aspect. Approx. height: 8–10ft (2.5–3m)
'Louise Rowe'	Pale lilac with cream stamens. Fully double, semi-double and single can often flower at the same time. Likes a semi-shaded location. Approx. height: 6½–8ft (2–2.5m)
'Margaret Wood'	White with reddish-brown anthers. Large flowers. Approx. height: 8–10ft (2.5–3m)
'Marie Boisselot' (ms)	White with gold stamens. Large flowers from late spring to late summer; vigorous. Approx. height: 10–13ft (3–4m)
'Masquerade'	Blue-mauve with rosy bars. Compact and very free-flowering. Approx. height: 6½–8ft (2–2.5m)
'Maureen' (ms)	Deep red-purple. Large flowers late spring to late summer. Compact. Free-flowering. Good for containers. Approx. height: 6½–8ft (2–2.5m)
'Miss Bateman'	White with reddish-brown stamens. Flowers mid- to late spring and occasionally later. Approx. height: 6½–8ft (2–2.5m)
'Monte Cassino'	Glowing red with cream stamens. Large flowers. Approx. height: 8–10ft (2.5–3m)
'Moonlight'	Cream with a hint of greenish-yellow. Plant in semi-shade for best colouring. Approx. height: 8–10ft (2.5–3m)
'Mrs Bush' (ms)	Pale mauve with beige anthers. Very large flowers late spring to late summer. Approx. height: 8–10ft (2.5–3m)
'Mrs Cholmondley' (ms)	Pale lavender-blue with mauve veining. Free-flowering mid-spring to late summer. Approx. height: 10–13ft (3–4m)
'Mrs George Jackman'	Creamy-white with pale brown anthers and white filaments. Semi-double flowers early, single later. Approx. height: 8–10ft (2.5–3m)
'Mrs Hope' (ms)	Bright blue with red stamens. Large flowers from late spring to late summer. Approx. height: 10–13ft (3–4m)
'Mrs James Mason'	Rich violet-blue with reddish-mauve stripes. Very large semi-double flowers early, single later. Approx. height: 6½–8ft (2–2.5m)
'Mrs N. Thompson'	Deep purple with very bright red stripe. Flowers mid- to late spring and mid-summer. Approx. height: 6½–8ft (2–2.5m)
'Mrs P. B. Truax'	Pale blue with cream stamens. Cup-shaped flowers. Approx. height: 8–10ft (2.5–3m)
'Multi Blue'	Deep blue with silver reverse. Large double, semi-double and single flowers, early and late. Approx. height: 6½–8ft (2–2.5m)
'Myojo'	Bluish-red with deep red stripes and cream stamens. Velvety texture. Approx. height: 6½–8ft (2–2.5m)
'Natacha'	Pale lilac-pink; deep mauve stripes; reddish-purple anthers. Large flowers. Approx. height: 6½–8ft (2–2.5m)
'Nelly Moser'	Pale mauve-pink flowers with striking pink stripes. Plant in north-facing site or in shade to protect flowers from fading. Approx. height: 9–13ft (3–4m)

ABOVE '**Patricia Ann Fretwell**' is a new double, early hybrid providing a spectacular show

'Patricia Ann Fretwell'	Pink with deeper pink edges. A new and stunning addition to the early double varieties. Approx. height: 6½–8ft (2–2.5m)
'Peveril Pearl'	Silvery-lilac with deeper bars. Plant in semi-shade to protect flowers from fading. Approx. height: 6½–8ft (2–2.5m)
'Prince Philip'	Rosy-mauve with reddish-pink bars. The tapering sepals have wavy edges. Approx. height: 8–10ft (2.5–3m)
'Princess of Wales' (ms)	Pale mauve. Large satin-like flowers late spring to late summer. Approx. height: 8–10ft (2.5–3m)
'Prins Hendrik' (ms)	Bright mauve-blue with purple anthers. Large flowers with wavy edges late spring to mid-summer. Approx. height: 6½–8ft (2–2.5m)
'Proteus'	Lilac-rose pink. Fully double flowers early, single later. Approx. height: 8–10ft (2.5–3m)
'Ramona'	Lavender-blue. Flowers have a satiny effect. Approx. height: 6½–8ft (2–2.5m)
'Richard Pennell'	Reddish-purple with gold anthers. Large flowers. Approx. height: 8–10ft (2.5–3m)
'Royalty'	Rosy-mauve with paler mauve-blue bars. Double flowers early, single later. Good choice for containers. Approx. height: 6½–8ft (2–2.5m)
'Royal Velvet'	Deep purple-blue with red anthers. Velvety effect. Good choice for containers. Approx. height: 6½–8ft (2–2.5m)

'Ruby Glow' (ms)   Mauve-red with ruby-red bars. Deep red anthers. Large flowers late spring to late summer. Approx. height: 8–10ft (2.5–3m)

'Saturn'   Lavender-blue with soft mauve bars. Very large flowers. Approx. height: 8–10ft (2.5–3m)

'Scartho Gem' (ms)   Bright pink with paler edges and deep anthers. Flowers late spring to late summer. A good choice for containers. Approx. height: 6½–8ft (2–2.5m)

'Sealand Gem' (ms)   Pale pearly grey-mauve with reddish-mauve stripes. Occasional semi-double on old wood; late spring to late summer. Approx. height: 8–10ft (2.5–3m)

'Serenata' (ms)   Deep purple with creamy-yellow stamens. Large flowers late spring to late summer. Approx. height: 8–10ft (2.5–3m)

'Sho-un' (ms)   Lavender-blue with deeper blue veins and white stamens. Very large flowers late spring to late summer. Approx. height: 6½–8ft (2–2.5m)

'Silver Moon' (ms)   Silver-grey with yellow stamens. Large flowers late spring to late summer. Approx. height: 8–10ft (2.5–3m)

'Sir Garnet Wolseley'   Mauve-purple with reddish-purple anthers. Compact and free-flowering. A good choice for containers. Approx. height: 6½–8ft (2–2.5m)

'Snow Queen'   White, initially tinged mauve, with red stamens. Large, wavy-edged flowers. Approx. height: 8–10ft (2.5–3m)

'Special Occasion' (ms)   Very pale pink with slightly deeper flush; reddish-brown anthers. Large flowers late spring to mid-summer. Approx. height: 6½–8ft (2–2.5m)

ABOVE **The delicately coloured *C.* 'Special Occasion' blooms between late spring and mid-summer**

'Sugar Candy' (ms)   Pink-mauve with deeper pink stripes and yellow anthers. Flowers late spring to late summer. Approx. height: 8–10ft (2.5–3m)

'Sunset' (ms)   Glowing mauve-red with bright golden-yellow stamens. Flowers late spring to late summer. Approx. height: 8–10ft (2.5–3m)

'Sylvia Denny'   White with creamy-yellow stamens. Double flowers early, single later. Strongly scented. Approx. height: 8–10ft (2.5–3m)

'Sympathia' (ms)   Rosy-mauve with reddish-brown stamens. Large flowers late spring to late summer. Approx. height: 6½–8ft (2–2.5m)

'The Bride' (ms)   White with cream stamens. Large flowers late spring to late summer. Approx. height: 6½–8ft (2–2.5m)

'The President' (ms)   Deep purple with red anthers. Large flowers late spring to late summer. Approx. height: 8–10ft (2.5–3m)

'The Vagabond'   Deep burgundy with purple stripes and creamy-yellow stamens. Very compact. Good for containers. Approx. height: 5–6½ft (1.5–2m)

'Titania' (ms)   White with reddish-pink stripes. Deep maroon anthers with white filaments. Exceptionally large flowers late spring to late summer. Approx. height: 8–10ft (2.5–3m)

'Twilight'   Mauve-pink fading at the edges; yellow stamens. Very free-flowering. Approx. height: 6½–8ft (2–2.5m)

ABOVE *C.* 'The President' was introduced in 1876 and is now one of the most popular hybrids

ABOVE *C. 'William Kennet'* has a lovely two-tone effect as the sepals fade

'Veronica's Choice'	Very pale lavender streaked with a very soft rosy-lilac. Double flowers in mid- to late spring. Plant in semi-shade. Approx. height: 8–10ft (2.5–3m)
'Vino'	Bright red with cream stamens. Flowers almost continuously from mid-spring to late summer. Approx. height: 8–10ft (2.5–3m)
'Violet Charm' (ms)	Intense violet-blue with red stamens. Flowers late spring to late summer. Approx. height: 6½–8ft (2–2.5m)
'Violet Elizabeth'	Mauve-pink. Double flowers early, single later. Approx. height: 6½–8ft (2–2.5m)
'Vyvyan Pennell'	Mauve-blue flushed with red. Large, fully double early flowers, single later. Approx. height: 8–10ft (2.5–3m)
'Wada's Primrose'	Creamy-yellow large flowers scented like satsumas. Approx. height: 6½–8ft (2–2.5m)
'Walter Pennell'	Greyish-mauve with carmine bars. Double flowers early, single later. Approx. height: 8–10ft (2.5–3m)
'W. E. Gladstone' (ms)	Lilac-blue with purple stamens. Exceptionally large flowers in late spring to late summer. Vigorous. Approx. height: 10–13ft (3–4m)
'Will Goodwin' (ms)	Pale lavender-blue with golden stamens. Wavy-edged flowers during late spring to late summer. Approx. height: 8–10ft (2.5–3m)
'William Kennet' (ms)	Deep mauve-blue with red stamens. The sun fades the flowers to give a lovely two-tone effect. Blooms all summer. Approx. height: 10–13ft (3–4m)

CATEGORY 3 CLEMATIS

C. texensis

Flowering season:	Early summer to early autumn, unless stated otherwise
Flowers:	Tulip shaped, ¾–1in (2–2.5cm) unless stated otherwise
Aspect:	Sunny and preferably sheltered. They love to scramble and climb over other plants
Cultivation:	Follow recommended planting, watering and feeding instructions outlined in Chapter 2
Pruning:	Hard prune, because flowers are formed on current year's growth. Like a perennial plant, they will naturally die down in late autumn
Background:	*Clematis texensis* was introduced from America in the latter part of the nineteenth century where it was found growing wild. The original species is still quite a rarity, but a number of hybrids have been raised to increase choice amongst these beautiful tulip-shaped, vibrantly coloured clematis
Popular varieties:	
texensis	Shades of red from deep cherry to vermilion and crimson. Small, urn-shaped flowers. Approx. height: 6½–8ft (2–2.5m)

ABOVE *C. texensis* species is a rare beauty

ABOVE 'Duchess of Albany' scrambles beautifully over evergreen shrub coprosma

'Duchess of Albany'   Candy-pink with deeper bars. Flowers face upward; a good variety for scrambling through low shrubs or for a container. Approx. height: 6½–8ft (2–2.5m)

'Etoile Rose'   Bright pink with silvery-pink margins. Good choice for growing over an archway. Approx. height: 8–10ft (2.5–3m)

'Gravetye Beauty'   Rich deep red with matching stamens. These upward-facing flowers open wider than type. Approx. height: 8–10ft (2.5–3m)

'Ladybird Johnson'   Purple-red with yellow stamens. Outward-facing flowers. Approx. height: 6½–8ft (2–2.5m)

'Pagoda'   White with pink-mauve edges and veining. Flowers larger than type; they have four sepals which recurve to resemble a pagoda. Approx. height: 6½–8ft (2–2.5m)

'Princess Diana'   Formerly called 'The Princess of Wales'. Deep vibrant pink with paler margins. Outward-facing, trumpet-shaped flowers during mid-summer to early autumn. Approx. height: 6½–8ft (2–2.5m)

'Sir Trevor Lawrence'   Red-purple outward-facing flowers with red stripes; sepals recurve slightly. Approx. height: 6½–8ft (2–2.5m)

'Viorna'   Reddish-purple urn-shaped flowers. A rare *texensis* type. Approx. height: 6½–8ft (2–2.5m)

C. viticella

Flowering season:	Early to late summer (unless stated otherwise)
Flowers:	Open, bell-shaped 1½–3in (4–8cm)
Aspect:	Any; particularly suited to growing through trees and shrubs, and a good choice for containers
Cultivation:	Follow recommended planting, watering and feeding instructions outlined in Chapter 2
Pruning:	If blooms are required low down, or space is limited, hard prune, because flowers are formed on current year's growth. If grown through trees or tall shrubs, *viticella* types can be left unpruned and allowed to scramble to their full height
Background:	*Clematis viticella* was introduced from Spain in the mid-sixteenth century. From the original species many cultivars and hybrids have been bred and continue to be raised by the many admirers of this valuable group

Popular varieties:

viticella	Mid-deep purple. Not widely grown even though it flowers profusely. Approx. height: 13–16½ft (4–5m)
'Abundance'	Red-pink flowers with deeper veins and creamy-green stamens. As the name suggests, a very free-flowering cultivar. Approx. height: 8–10ft (2.5–3m)
'Alba Luxurians'	White flowers with green-tipped sepals and deep purplish-black anthers. Attractive and unusual flower formation. Approx. height: 8–10ft (2.5–3m)
'Betty Corning'	Creamy-white, edged and veined in pale lilac. Very free-flowering and sweetly scented. Approx. height: 8–10ft (2.5–3m)
'Black Prince'	Purple-black with green stamens. Flowers grow in more upright manner than type. Approx. height: 8–10ft (2.5–3m)
'Blue Belle'	Deep purple with cream anthers. Larger flowers than type. Approx. height: 10–13ft (3–4m)
'Elvan'	Purple flowers with cream stripes. Very free-flowering. Approx. height: 10–13ft (3–4m)
'Entel'	Light violet with dark veins. Pale greenish-yellow anthers. A good companion for roses. Approx. height: 6½–10ft (2–3m)
'Etoile Violette'	Deep purple with creamy-yellow stamens. Very free-flowering. Approx. height: 10–13ft (3–4m)
'Foxtrot'	White flowers edged in bluish-purple. A new cultivar that is ideal for growing through medium-sized shrubs. Approx. height: 8–10ft (2.5–3m)
'Kermesina'	Deep wine-red with a white spot at the base of each sepal. Very free-flowering. Approx. height: 10–13ft (3–4m)
'Little Nell'	Small white dainty flowers edged in pale mauve; green stamens. Approx. height: 10–13ft (3–4m)

'Madame Julia Correvon'	Rich vibrant red flowers with golden stamens and twisted sepals. Larger flowers than type. Approx. height: 8–10ft (2.5–3m)
'Margot Koster'	Mauve-pink. Open appearance with twisted sepals. Approx. height: 8–10ft (2.5–3m)
'Mary Rose'	(*Viticella* 'Flore Pleno'.) Deep greyish-purple. This cultivar is believed to be very old; known as *C. peregrina purpurea flore plena* in 1623 and the 'double purple virgins bower' when described in 1629. Re-introduced and re-named in recent years as 'Mary Rose'. Approx. height: 8–10ft (2.5–3m)
'Minuet'	Cream, edged in rosy-mauve; green stamens. Grows well in any aspect. Approx. height: 8–10ft (2.5–3m)
'Polish Spirit'	Rich purple-red with deep red anthers. Easy to grow. Masses of blooms. Approx. height: 10–13ft (3–4m)
'Purpurea Plena Elegans'	Dusky purple. Double flowers in profusion. Similar to 'Flora Pleno' ('Mary Rose'). Approx. height: 10–13ft (3–4m)
'Royal Velours'	Deep reddish-purple with matching anthers. Grows well in any aspect. Approx. height: 10–13ft (3–4m)

ABOVE *C. viticella* **'Madame Julia Correvon'**

'Rubra'	Deep crimson with brown stamens. Flowers in profusion. Approx. height: 8–10ft (2.5–3m)
'Soldertalje'	Reddish-pink nodding flowers with green anthers. Approx. height: 10–13ft (3–4m)
'Tango'	Cream flowers, edged and veined in red. Similar to 'Minuet' but brighter. Approx. height: 8–10ft (2.5–3m)
'Venosa Violacea'	White flowers, edged and veined in purple with very deep purple anthers. Flowers than type. Approx. height: 8–10ft (2.5–3m)

Herbaceous species and cultivars

Flowering season:	Varies between late spring and late autumn
Flowers:	Various shapes and sizes as stated
Aspect:	Suitable for planting in a mixed border. They will generally tolerate any aspect
Cultivation:	Follow recommended planting, watering and feeding instructions outlined in Chapter 2
Pruning:	Most herbaceous clematis fit into Category 3. Like other herbaceous plants they naturally die back in the winter and only need to be trimmed and neatened. Small rockery plants which bloom early in the season may not require pruning and this will be stated
Background:	Herbaceous clematis are mostly resultant of breeding from the species *integrifolia*, *recta* and *heracleifolia*. *Integrifolia* and *recta* were introduced from Europe in the latter part of the sixteenth century. *Heracleifolia* was discovered in northern China just into the second half of the nineteenth century. In the following list, the herbaceous clematis have been roughly grouped together by type

Popular species and varieties:

integrifolia	Indigo-blue with twisted, recurving sepals. Sweetly scented nodding flowers late spring to late summer. Approx. height: 2–3¼ft (0.5–1m)
'Alba'	Pure white flowers during late spring to late summer. Approx. height: 2–3¼ft (0.5–1m)
'Amy'	Silvery-white, sky-blue on the inside. Sweetly scented. Blooms late spring to late summer. Approx. height: 2–3¼ft (0.5–1m)
'Floris V'	Burgundy sweetly scented flowers in late spring to late summer. Approx. height: 2–3¼ft (0.5–1m)
eriostemon 'Hendersonii'	Deep blue star-shaped flowers in profusion during early to late summer. Approx. height: 5–6½ft (1.5–2m)
'Lauren'	Deep lilac flowers that are edged in paler lilac-pink. Sweetly scented. Blooms late spring to late summer. Approx. height: 2–3½ft (1.5–1m)
'Olgae'	Mid-blue sweetly scented flowers with twisted sepals. Blooms late spring to late summer. Approx. height: 2–3½ft (1.5–1m)

ABOVE **Herbaceous clematis scramble through border and die back naturally**

'Pangbourne Pink'	Deep cerise-pink nodding flowers during late spring to late summer. Approx. height: 2–3½ft (1.5–1m)
'Pastel Blue'	Pale powder blue. Blooms late spring to late summer. Approx. height: 2–3½ft (0.5–1m)
'Pastel Pink'	Flesh-pink nodding flowers with twisted recurving sepals. Blooms late spring to late summer. Approx. height: 2–3½ft (1.5–1m)
'Rosea'	Bright pink. Sweetly scented. Blooms late spring to late summer. Approx. height: 2–3¼ft (1.5–1m)
'Tapestry'	Deep pink, late spring to late summer. Approx. height: 2–3¼ft (1.5–1m)
heracleifolia davidiana	Lavender-blue Hyacinth-like, sweetly scented. Blooms late spring to late summer. Approx. height: 3¼–5ft (1–1.5m)
'Aljonushka'	Rose-pink nodding flowers from late spring to late summer. Approx. height: 5–6½ft (1.5–2m)
'Arabella'	Purple-blue with cream anthers. Good choice for containers or growing through small shrubs. Approx. height: 5–6½ft (1.5–2m)
'Aromatica'	Deep violet-blue with yellow stamens. Needs sunny border. Sweetly scented. Late spring to late summer. Approx. height: 5–6½ft (1.5–2m)
'Campanile'	Pale blue with paler bars. Hyacinth-like flowers, late spring to late summer. Approx. height: 5–6½ft (1.5–2m)
'Cote d'Azur'	Pale blue small flowers with white bars. Blooms late spring to late summer. Approx. height: 5–6½ft (1.5–2m)

'Crepuscule' Small pale mauve tubular flowers. Scented. Early to late summer. Approx. height: 3¼–5ft (1–1.5m)

brachyura White with cream stamens. Small scented flowers in profusion. A rare species from Korea. Late spring to mid-summer. Approx. height: 5–6½ft (1.5–2m)

'Durandii' Indigo-blue with bright yellow stamens. A lovely clematis to grow through small shrubs and roses in the border. Late spring to late summer. Approx. height: 6½–8ft (2–2.5m)

'Edward Pritchard' Cream flowers, edged with caramel, in early to late summer. Needs full sun to draw out the scent. Approx. height: 5–6½ft (1.5–2m)

hirsutissima var. *scottii* Lavender-blue urn-shaped flowers with cream stamens. Needs a sunny aspect. A rare species from the Rockies, USA. Blooms late spring to mid-summer. Approx. height: 6½–8ft (2–2.5m)

ispahanica Small white flowers with deep red stamens and recurving sepals. From Iran. Approx. height: 5–6½ft (1.5–2m)

'Joe' (formerly *cartmanii* 'Joe') White. Small flowers in profusion in early spring. Evergreen, finely cut foliage. Good for rockery, in sun. Needs winter protection. Category 1: do not prune. Approx. height: 2ft (0.5m)

jouiniana Pale mauve. Flowers in large panicles, early to late summer. Good ground cover. Approx. height: 6½–8ft (2–2.5m)

jouiniana 'Praecox' Mauve-pink. An earlier-flowering form of 'Jouiniana'. Blooms late spring to late summer. Approx. height: 6½–8ft (2–2.5m)

mandshurica White, star-shaped flowers with an aniseed scent, in profusion, early to late summer. Approx. height: 5–6½ft (1.5–2m)

ABOVE *C.* 'Durandii' will scramble through the border or climb to 8ft (2.5m) if given support

'Mrs Robert Brydon'	Grey-blue. A small, subtle flower. Blooms mid- to late summer. Approx. height: 6½–8ft (2–2.5m)
'Petit Faucon'	Deep violet with yellow anthers. Semi-nodding flowers during early to late summer. Approx. height: 3¼–5ft (1–1.5m)
recta	Pure white, sweetly scented flowers in profusion during late spring to mid-summer. Needs support. Approx. height: 5–6½ft (1.5–2m)
'Peveril'	Pure white scented flowers late spring to mid-summer. More compact than *recta*. Approx. height: 3¼–5ft (1–1.5m)
'Purpurea'	White, scented flowers during late spring to mid-summer. Approx. height: 5–6½ft (1.5–2m)
songarica	Pure white with yellow stamens. Flowers early to mid-summer, followed by attractive seed heads. Bamboo-like stems. Native of Siberia and Mongolia, introduced in late nineteenth century. Approx. height: 3¼–5ft (1–1.5m)
stans	Tiny blue tubular flowers in profusion during mid-summer to early autumn. Requires full sun to draw out the lily-of-the-valley scent. A rare species. Approx. height: 3¼–5ft (1–1.5m)
'Rusalka'	Bright Wedgwood-blue. All of the beauty of *stans*, but with more delicate foliage and a dwarf habit. Approx. height: 3¼ft (1m)
versicolor	Deep cherry-pink tips and white base. Small urn-shaped flowers early to late summer; striking seed heads. Rare species introduced from USA in late nineteenth century. Approx. height: 5–6½ft (1.5–2m)

Late, large-flowered cultivars

Flowering season:	Early to late summer; mid-season varieties: late spring to late summer
Flowers:	Mostly saucer-shaped, 4–5½in (10–14cm) unless stated otherwise
Aspect:	Any (unless stated otherwise)
Cultivation:	Follow recommended planting, watering, and feeding instructions outlined in Chapter 2
Pruning:	Hard prune, because flowers are formed on current year's growth. Mid-season varieties: optional, hard prune or partial prune according to requirements. The mid-season hybrids shown in this category generally need a hard prune periodically to prevent them from becoming leggy. Please note that mid-season varieties are marked 'ms'
Background:	Clematis within this group, like those of the early, large-flowered hybrids, are the result of breeding by clematis enthusiasts and specialists from many parts of the world. Most have been introduced during the past century. Unlike the early-flowering hybrids, however, choice is somewhat restricted
Popular varieties:	
'Ascotiensis' (ms)	Bright lavender-blue. Usually in flower during Ascot week. Late spring to late summer. Approx. height: 10–13ft (3–4m)

ABOVE *C. florida* 'Alba Plena'

'Bella'	White, initially with cream stripes. Compact and free-flowering. Good choice for containers. Approx. height: 6½–8ft (2–2.5m)
'Black Prince'	Deepest shade of purple, almost black, fading to reddish-purple. 10–13ft (3–4m)
'Blue Angel' (Blekitny Aniol)	Sky-blue, with slightly darker edges. Sepals deeply furrowed with wavy edges. Approx. height: 10–13ft (3–4m)
'Cardinal Wyszynski' (ms)	Crimson. Vigorous; flowers in profusion late spring to late summer. Approx. height: 8–10ft (2.5–3m)
'Comtesse de Bouchard'	Mauve-pink. Flowers in profusion. Approx. height: 10–13ft (3–4m)
'Dorothy Walton'	Mauve with pink-mauve mottling. Long, pointed sepals. Approx. height: 10–13ft (3–4m)
florida 'Alba Plena' (ms)	Greenish-white. Fully double flowers; likes sunny position away from winds. A good choice for containers. Flowers late spring to late summer. Approx. height: 6½–8ft (2–2.5m)
florida 'Sieboldii' (ms)	White with deep purple centres. Exotic, tender variety; ideal for container on patio or conservatory. Flowers late spring to late summer. Approx. height: 6½–8ft (2–2.5m)
'Gipsy Queen'	Deep purple with red anthers. Flowers in abundance; they have a velvet sheen. Approx. height: 10–13ft (3–4m)

'Guiding Star'	Violet-blue. Nicely shaped flowers. Approx. height: 8–10ft (2.5–3m)
'Hagley Hybrid'	Pale mauve-pink with reddish-brown anthers. Plant in shade to protect colouring. Approx. height: 6½ft (2m)
'Huldine'	Pearly-white with pale pink on reverse. Thrives in full sun. Approx. height: 10–13ft (3–4m)
'Jackmanii'	Deep purple with green stamens. Very free-flowering. Approx. height: 10–13ft (3–4m)
'Jenny Caddick'	Reddish-mauve with cream stamens. A recent introduction. Approx. height: 8–10ft (2.5–3m)
'John Huxtable'	White with creamy-yellow stamens. Very free-flowering. Approx. height: 8–10ft (2.5–3m)
'Lady Betty Balfour'	Deep blue with creamy-yellow stamens. Plant in full sun for a long season; mid-summer to early autumn. Approx. height: 10ft+ (3m+)
'Madame Baron Veillard'	Lilac-pink with greenish-white stamens. Plant in full sun for a long season; mid-summer to early autumn. Approx. height: 10ft+ (3m+)
'Madame Edouard André'	Deep wine-red with cream stamens. Prefers a southerly aspect. Approx. height: 10–13ft (3–4m)
'Madame Grangé'	Deep rosy-purple with reddish-purple anthers. Edges of the sepals curl inwards. Approx. height: 8–10ft (2.5–3m)
'Margaret Hunt'	Mauve-pink with reddish-brown anthers. Vigorous and free-flowering. Approx. height: 10–13ft (3–4m)
'Monte Cassino'	Glowing red with cream stamens. May fade in strong sunlight, good light required, not a north wall. Approx. height: 8–10ft (2.5–3m)
'Niobe'	Very deep red, almost black on opening; yellow stamens. A good variety for lovers of very dark flowers. Blooms late spring to late summer. Approx. height: 8–10ft (2.5–3m)
'Perle d'Azur'	Light blue with pale greenish-yellow stamens. Very vigorous and free-flowering. Approx. height: 10–13ft (3–4m)
'Perrins Pride'	Purple with bronze anthers. Leave some stems unpruned, as this variety produces larger flowers from old wood. Approx. height: 8–10ft (2.5–3m)
'Pink Fantasy'	Pale pink with deeper pink stripes and brown anthers. Wavy-edged sepals. Approx. height: 6½–8ft (2–2.5ft)
'Prince Charles'	Mauve-blue semi-nodding flowers on a free-flowering, compact plant. Good choice for containers. Approx. height: 6½–8ft (2–2.5ft)
'Rouge Cardinal' (ms)	Velvet-red with beige anthers. Flowers in profusion late spring to late summer. Approx. height: 6½–8ft (2–2.5ft)
'Star of India' (ms)	Deep purple with vivid red stripes. Flowers in profusion from late spring to late summer. Approx. height: 10–13ft (3–4m)
'Victoria' (ms)	Lilac-pink with buff stamens. Flowers late spring to early autumn. Approx. height: 10–13ft (3–4m)
'Ville de Lyon' (ms)	Bright red, fading in the sun to silvery pink edged in red; gold stamens. Flowers late spring to late summer. 10–13ft (3–4m)

'Viola'	Bluish-violet medium-sized flowers with greenish-yellow stamens. Approx. height: 8–10ft (2.5–3m)
'Vivienne Lawson'	Violet-purple with gold anthers and pointed sepals. Approx. height: 8–10ft (2.5–3m)
'Voluceau' (ms)	Petunia-red with yellow anthers. Very free-flowering late spring to late summer. Approx. height: 8–10ft (2.5–3m)
'Warsaw Nike'	Very deep purple with cream stamens. Another very dark variety. Approx. height: 8–10ft (2.5–3m)
'Westerplatte' (ms)	Dark velvet-red with red stamens and yellow anthers; mid-spring to late summer. Distinctive velvety sheen. Approx. height: 3¼ft (1m)

Late, small-flowered species and cultivars

Flowering season:	Varies between late spring and early autumn
Flowers:	Mostly small, of various shapes, as stated
Aspect:	Any, unless stated otherwise
Cultivation:	Follow recommended planting, watering and feeding instructions outlined in Chapter 2
Pruning:	Hard prune, because flowers are formed on current year's growth
Background:	There are a number of species within this group and the background, where known, is detailed. There are a few rare and unusual varieties, which will appeal to the rare plant collector, but the mass of sweetly scented blooms for long summer months makes them a delightful addition to any garden
Popular varieties:	
'Annemieke'	Small yellow nodding flowers with twisted recurving sepals; early to late summer. Raised in Holland during recent years. Approx. height: 10–13ft (3–4m)
apilifolia	Creamy-white with prominent cream stamens and bright green foliage. The small, star-shaped flowers bloom in profusion. Introduced from China during the late nineteenth century. Approx. height: 13–16½ft (4–5m)
buchananiana	Creamy-yellow. Plant in sun to enhance small, scented flowers which grow in profusion, mid-summer to early autumn. From the Himalayas. Approx. height: 16½–19½ft (5–6m)
'Burford Bell'	Pale purple-blue. Small, nodding flowers early summer to early autumn. Approx. height: 8–10ft (2.5–3m)
campaniflora	White, tinged with blue. Dainty, nodding flowers early to late summer. Species from Portugal during the early nineteenth century. Approx. height: 10–13ft (3–4m)
chinensis	Small white star-shaped flowers that bloom from early to late summer. Best to plant in a sunny aspect to draw out the sweet scent. From China during the mid-eighteenth century. Approx. height: 10–13ft (3–4m)

connata	Small yellow bell-shaped flowers with big, veined leaves. Sweet scent. Sunny aspect. From Tibet during the late nineteenth century. Approx. height: 19½ft (6m)
crispa	Violet-blue, star-shaped, white inside. Small, bell-shaped flowers early to late summer, then spider-like seed heads. From America during early eighteenth century. Approx. height: 5–6½ft (1.5–2m)
crispa hybrid	(Not yet named.) Dusky mauve-red; paler at the base of the sepals. Flowers larger than *crispa*, early to late summer. Approx. height: 10–13ft (3–4m)
'Cylindrica'	Mauve-blue nodding flowers early to late summer. Hybrid of *integrifolia* and *crispa*. Approx. height: 3¼–5ft (1–1.5m)
flammula	Small pure white star-shaped flowers, early summer to early autumn. Prune back by half. Plant in full sun. From southern Europe during the end of the sixteenth century. Approx. height: 13–16½ft (4–5m)
fusca	Small chocolate-brown urn-shaped flowers with short brown hairs; late spring to late summer, then attractive seed heads. From north-east Asia mid-nineteenth century. Approx. height: 6½–8ft (2–2.5m)

ABOVE Almond-scented *flammula* will flower from early summer to early autumn in a sunny border

149

fusca violacea	Purple, small, urn-shaped flowers in late spring to late summer, followed by striking seed heads. Introduced from north China during late nineteenth century. Approx. height: 6½–8ft (2–2.5m)
gouriana	Creamy-white small flowers mid-summer to early autumn. Vigorous. From Nepal. Approx. height: 13–16½ft (4–5m)
'Grace'	(A hybrid of *serratifolia* x *ligusticifolia*.) Creamy-white with wine-red stamens. Flowers are held on long stalks. Originally raised in Canada early twentieth century. Approx. height: 10–11½ft (3–3.5m)
grata	Creamy-white small flowers mid-summer to early autumn. A rare species from China and Taiwan at the start of the twentieth century. Approx. height: 26ft (8m)
hilariae	Bright yellow outward-facing flowers with twisted, recurving sepals early to late summer. Attractive seed heads. Rare, from Afghanistan. Approx. height: 10–16½ft (3–5m)
intricata (akebiodes)	Creamy-yellow, flushed maroon at base, nodding flowers with twisted, recurving sepals during late spring to late summer. From China. Approx. height: 10ft (3m)
kirilowii	White, small, scented flowers early to late summer. Likes sunny position. Native of China. Approx. height: 10–13ft (3–4m)
ladakhiana	Gold with bronze speckles. Small, nodding flowers with twisted, recurving sepals, mid-summer to early autumn. From Kashmir. Approx. height: 10–13ft (3–4m)
lasiandra	Reddish-purple, small, nodding flowers with recurving sepals. mid- to late summer. Species found wild in Japan, China and Taiwan. Approx. height: 6½–8ft (2–2.5m)
ligusticifolia	White, small, star-shaped flowers, in profusion, early to late summer. North American species. Approx. height: 19½ft (6m)
'Lisboa'	Pale mauve. Small flowers with recurving sepals. Early to late summer. Approx. height: 8–10ft (2.5–3m)
'Paul Farges' (Summer Snow)	White, small, sweetly scented flowers in profusion, early to late summer. Raised in Ukraine. Approx. height: 16½–19½ft (5–6m)
peterae	Creamy-white, small, scented flowers. Requires sunny position. From China. Approx. height: 16½ft (5m)
pierotii	White small flowers, mid-summer to early autumn. Sunny position to prolong flowering. Rare, from Japan. Approx. height: 10–13ft (3–4m)
pitcheri	Deep pink-red on the outside, deep red inside. Urn-shaped nodding flowers, curled-back sepals. From west of America. Approx. height: 6½–8ft (2–2.5m)
potanini	White with yellow anthers. Flowers late spring to late summer. Small, silvery seed heads. Approx. height: 10–16½ft (3–5m)
rehderiana	Straw-yellow with bright yellow stamens. Large panicles of small cowslip-like flowers, with a similar fragrance, early to late summer. Sunny position. From west China during the twentieth century. Approx. height: 19½ft (6m)

ABOVE *C. x triternata* 'Rubro-marginata' has a dainty flower with a light, marzipan fragrance

serratifolia	Pale lemon-yellow small flowers with a lemon scent, early summer to early autumn, followed by attractive seed heads. From Korea at beginning of twentieth century. Approx. height: 13–16½ft (4–5m)
terniflora	White, small, scented flowers with hosta-like leaves, mid- to late summer. Sunny position. Vigorous. From China and Japan. Approx. height: 26ft (8m)
thunbergii	White with creamy-yellow stamens. Small, sweetly scented flowers with recurving sepals, in profusion, mid-summer to early autumn. Approx. height: 10–13ft (3–4m)
x *triternata* 'Rubro-marginata'	Bright mauve-pink fading to white at base. Masses of small flowers with a marzipan scent, early to late summer. Raised nineteenth century, *flammula* x *viticella*. Approx. height: 10–13ft (3–4m)
veitchiana	Straw-yellow. A relative of *rehderiana*. Sweet scent. Plant in sun. From China early twentieth century. Approx. height: 19½ft (6m)
viorna	Mauve-pink with cream inner. Nodding flowers, recurving sepals, early to late summer. From east America during the early eighteenth century. Approx. height: 6½–8ft (2–2.5m)

virginiana	White with cream stamens. Small, sweetly scented flowers, large, deep bronze young leaves. Mid-summer to early autumn. From America mid-eighteenth century. Approx. height: 13–16½ft (4–5m)
vitalba (Old Man's Beard)	Creamy-white, initially tinged green. Britain's native clematis. Flowers are followed by masses of seed heads. Early to late summer. Approx. height: 19½–26ft (6–8m)
'Western Virgin'	Pure white with yellow anthers. Small flowers in profusion, early to late summer. A vigorous hybrid. Approx. height: 36ft (11m)

The *orientalis* group

Flowering season:	Early to late summer, unless stated otherwise
Flowers:	Nodding bell-shaped or open bell-shaped, followed by attractive seed heads, ¾–1½in (2–4cm)
Aspect:	Sun or semi-shade
Cultivation:	Follow recommended planting, watering and feeding instructions outlined in Chapter 2
Pruning:	Pruning is optional. An effective method, however, is to prune half the stems to the ground in early spring. The unpruned stems will then have flowers at their full height while the new stems will flower low down
Background:	Because of their nodding bell-shaped flowers in various shades of yellow, the following clematis have been grouped together. They are made up of *orientalis*, *tangutica* and *tibetana* species and their cultivars and hybrids. Due to cross-breeding it is difficult to allocate them specifically. *Clematis tangutica* was introduced in the late nineteenth century having been found growing wild from north-west India to west China. *Clematis tibetana* was introduced a few years later and as the name suggests its homeland was Tibet. *Clematis orientalis* is a species from Afghanistan
Popular varieties:	
'Aureolin'	Lemon-yellow. Flowers open wider than type. Approx. height: 13–16½ft (4–5m)
'Bill Mackenzie'	Strong yellow. Larger flowers than type with recurving tips, followed by very large, fluffy seed heads. Approx. height: 13–16½ft (4–5m)
'Burford Variety'	Deep yellow. Silvery seed heads. Approx. height: 10–13ft (3–4m)
'Golden Harvest'	Yellow with purple stamens. Small, nodding flowers. Approx. height: 10–13ft (3–4m)
'Helios'	Bright yellow nodding flowers opening flat from mid- to late summer. Very free-flowering; of low growth. Approx. height: 5–6½ft (1.5–2m)
'Laciniifolia'	Orange-yellow with maroon stamens. Small, nodding flowers. Approx. height: 13–16½ft (4–5m)
'Lambton Park'	Bright yellow. Large flowers followed by large seed heads. Approx. height: 13–16½ft (4–5m)

'Orange Peel'	Orange-yellow, small, nodding flowers. Approx. height: 13–16½ft (4–5m)
tangutica	Mid-yellow. Vigorous growth with abundant flowers, followed by large, fluffy seed heads. Approx. height: 13–16½ft (4–5m)
tibetana	Pale yellow small, nodding flowers. Approx. height: 13–16½ft (4–5m)
var. *tenuifolia*	Bright yellow small, nodding flowers with reflexed sepals on long stalks. Mid-summer to early autumn. Approx. height: 10–13ft (3–4m)
'Vernayi L & S 13342'	Yellow small, nodding flowers with very thick sepals. Approx. height: 13–16½ft (4–5m)
x *glauca akebiodes*	Orange-yellow with brown stamens. Flowers open almost fully with lovely blue-green foliage. Approx. height: 10–13ft (3–4m)

ABOVE *Clematis* 'Bill Mackenzie' tumbles gracefully through *Escallonia* 'Iveyi'

Glossary

Acid Soil with a pH value below 7

Alkaline Soil with a pH value above 7

Annual A plant that completes its life cycle in one growing season, usually referring to summer bedding plants

Anther The upper part of the stamen that contains the pollen

Bed Area of ground, usually cultivated, in which plants are grown

Berry The fruit of plants made up of soft flesh surrounding seeds

Bisexual Refers to a plant with both male and female reproductive organs

Bract A modified leaf-like structure, which can sometimes appear petal-like, that grows between the leaf and stem

Calyx The collective name for the outer whorl of sepals

Chlorosis A loss of chlorophyll (a green pigment that absorbs energy from sunlight) caused by a mineral deficiency, poor light levels or disease

Corolla The collective name for petals

Cultivar A plant that is artificially raised or selected and its characteristics can be maintained by propagation

Deciduous A plant that sheds its leaves annually at the end of its growing season.

Ericaceous A plant belonging to the Ericaceae family. Describes potting compost with a pH of 6.5 or less in which acid-loving plants can be grown

Evergreen A plant that retains its leaves for more than one growing season

Foliar feed A diluted solution of fertilizer, normally sprayed onto plants, which then absorbs the nutrients through its leaves

Frost hardy A plant that is able to withstand temperatures down to 23°F (−5°C)

Friable soil Soil that is easily broken up, crumbly texture

Frost tender Temperatures below 41°F (5°C) may cause damage

Fully hardy A plant that is able to withstand temperatures down to 5°F (−15°C)

Fungicide An agent, usually a chemical, that destroys or helps to prevent fungal disease.

Fungus A mould or mushroom that survives by absorbing nutrients and organic material from its surroundings

Genus A family or plant species that share a wide range of characteristics

Ground frost This occurs when the temperature at soil level, or just below the surface, falls to 32°F (0°C)

Humus Organic material that has slowly decomposed. Also refers to rotted garden compost or leaf mould, which can be dug into the soil to improve texture

Hybrid Naturally or artificially produced offspring of at least two different varieties of plants. They can be similar to their parents or bear no resemblance at all. Successful hybridization combines the best qualities of each parent plant

Internode The part of a stem between two nodes (leaf joints)

Layering A method of propagation where the stem of a plant is pegged down into the soil to encourage rooting while it is still attached to the parent plant

Loam Earth that usually contains equal parts of sand, clay and silt, producing a highly fertile, well-drained, humus-rich soil

Node A joint at the stem of a plant, which is sometimes swollen, from which leaf buds and shoots are formed

Ovoid Egg-shaped with the broader end at the base

Perennial A plant that lives for more than two growing seasons

Petal The corolla of a flower, really a modified leaf, that is brightly coloured to attract insects

pH A measure of acidity or alkalinity. A wide range of plants prefer neutral or slightly acid soil of pH 5.5 to 7.5

Pinch out Sometimes referred to as stop. To remove soft-growing points to encourage the bushy growth of side shoots

Pistil The female reproductive organ of a plant, consisting of one or several carpels which may be joined

Pollen Grains of the anthers containing the male element necessary for fertilization

Pollination The transfer of pollen to the stigma. Insects and animals perform this operation but it can be done by hand

Recurving Curving or bending back or down.

Reflexed Arched or bent back upon itself

Sepal Part of the calyx. Sepals are often green and form as a protective shield for the petals, they fold back as the buds open. Sometimes the sepals are colourful and petal-like and the flower is formed by a whorl of sepals alone

Species A group of plants where the flowers and foliage are of the plants original habit and these characteristics differentiate them from another group

Stamen The male part of a flower

Systemic Mostly used to describe a type of insecticide which is absorbed by the plant, making it toxic to pests while still preserving the health of the plant

Tendril On climbing plants, a coiling leaflet or shoot used to attach itself to a support

Tepal The petals and sepals of a flower, which often whorl around together, making it difficult to separate them

Whorl A circular arrangement of leaves, petals, sepals, tepals or shoots, arising from a single point

Useful contacts

Contact your national clematis society for further information and a list of local suppliers.

American Clematis Society
c/o Edith Malek
P.O. Box 17085
Irvine,
CA 92623-7085
Tel. 949-224-9885
Email: edith@clematis.org
Web: www.clematis.org

British Clematis Society
2 Gatley Avenue
West Ewell
Surrey KT19 9NG
Tel. +44 (0)1276 476387
Email: postmaster@britishclematis.org.uk
Web: www.britishclematis.org.uk

International Clematis Society
3 Cuthberts Close
Goffs Oak
Hertfordshire EN7 5RB
Tel: +44 (0)1953 850407
Web: www.clematisinternation.com

About the author

Marigold Badcock discovered the joy of gardening when she and her husband Edward renovated the neglected garden of their first home; the design was to change many times during their twenty-year stay.

Now retired and living in the heart of the north Devon countryside in southwest England, Marigold shares her love of gardening and photography in this, her second book for GMC Publications; being an updated and abridged edition of her first book for GMC entitled *Companions to Clematis*.

Index

Pages highlighted in **bold** indicate photographs of plants

GMC Publications
Castle Place, 166 High Street, Lewes, East Sussex, BN7 1XU, United Kingdom
Tel: 01273 488005 Fax: 01273 402866
Website: www.gmcbooks.com
Contact us for a complete catalogue, or visit our website.
Orders by credit card are accepted.